The Runner's Diary

A DAILY TRAINING LOG

MATT FITZGERALD

VELO
press

BOULDER, COLORADO

3002 Sterling Circle, Suite 100
Boulder, Colorado 80301-2338 USA
(303) 440-0601 · Fax (303) 444-6788 · E-mail velopress@competitorgroup.com

Distributed in the United States and Canada by Ingram Publisher Services

Library of Congress Cataloging-in-Publication Data
Fitzgerald, Matt
    The runner's diary: a daily training log / Matt Fitzgerald.
        p. cm.
    ISBN 978-1-934030-36-3 (pbk.)
    1. Running—Training. 2. Exercise. 3. Physical fitness. 4. Runners (Sports)—Nutrition.
I. Title

GV1061.5.F574   2008
613.7'172—dc223
                                        2008044061

For information on purchasing VeloPress books, please call (800) 811-4210 ext. 2138 or visit www.velopress.com.

Front cover photo © Tim De Frisco
Back cover photo © Chris Milliman
Back cover photo © Robb Kendrick
Photo on p. 27 by Don Karle

13 14 / 10 9 8 7 6

CONTENTS

Introduction

The training diary is a runner's tradition that has been around for many decades. It goes at least as far back as Alfred Shrubb, a legendary English runner born in 1878 who kept detailed notes about his workouts and even published a book on his training methods.

The impulse to keep a training log is a natural one for runners. Running 20, 30, or 40 or more miles per week, month after month, is a significant accomplishment, but it's not like building a house—we can't see and touch our accomplishments as runners. If you're like me, you probably can't even remember most of the runs you've done. Keeping a training diary makes our running achievements more concrete and less ephemeral.

Pride is only one motivation for keeping a training diary, however. There are certainly other good reasons to do so. The simple effort of keeping such a diary increases our mental and emotional investment in the sport in ways that may positively affect our performance. And, of course, the information that we record can be very useful.

The usefulness of keeping a training diary underlies my recommendation that every runner keep one, regardless of how strongly he or she feels the impulse to do so (not all runners feel it equally). So I'm glad that you've picked up this training diary, and you'll soon be glad you did too. There are five specific ways in which it will help you become a better runner and find more satisfaction in your running.

Training analysis. A training diary helps you determine how well your training regimen is working. It does so by enabling you to connect cause and effect, where the cause is your workouts and the effect is your changing fitness level. By looking back over the information in your training diary, you can determine whether you need to run more mileage or less, whether you need more speed work or less, and so forth. There is always a way to train more effectively than you are doing today. Keeping a training diary makes it easier to find better ways to train.

Self-knowledge. Each runner is unique. Therefore, no two runners can get their best results by training in exactly the same way. One of your most important duties as a runner is to learn about your running self so you can use this self-knowledge to refine your training recipe. Your training diary provides a wealth of information through which to develop such self-knowledge. For example, in looking back over the past year's entries, it might strike you that your body seemed to respond much more quickly to speed work than it did to endurance training. You might use this knowledge to slightly shift the balance of your future training toward endurance in order to bolster an apparent weakness while maintaining an existing strength.

Motivation and accountability. Training can be a real grind. It takes a long time and a lot of hard work to build peak fitness for an important race. It is difficult to consistently maintain a high level of motivation throughout this process, and the price you pay for losing your motivation can be severe. Your training diary can help you avoid motivational dips by reinforcing your investment in your goals. It's a source of accountability because it holds you to the standards you have set for yourself as a runner. When you look back over all the training you have done, you can't help but think, "I can't stop now. Look at how much work I've done already! I owe it to myself to keep my momentum going until the very end."

Troubleshooting. Things inevitably go wrong in the training process. You develop injuries, you experience flat weeks, you have bad races, and so forth. Figuring out the cause of each setback will help you reduce the number of future setbacks you experience. Your training diary holds much of the information you need to successfully troubleshoot your setbacks. For example, in looking over your training diary during a period of injury, you might discover that you tend to get injured anytime you increase your weekly running mileage above a certain amount. Armed with this information, you can hold yourself below the danger level in the future and minimize your injuries.

Confidence building. Every runner experiences doubts about his or her ability to achieve race goals. The runners who most often achieve their goals are those who muster the confidence to shout down these natural voices of doubt. Your training diary can be a great source of confidence because it is a rich record of how much hard work you've accomplished and how much progress you've made. It is the nearest thing you have to proof that you can achieve your goals before you actually achieve them. Whenever you hear those voices of doubt within you, pick up your training diary and remind yourself of how much cause you have to believe that you will achieve your goals.

Like training itself, keeping a training diary rewards you in direct proportion to your investment in it. To get the most out of this training diary, you must record detailed, accurate information consistently, and you must use it for the five purposes discussed here. You've taken the first step in choosing this training diary. Now take the next!

[1] How to Use This Training Diary

If you've kept training diaries before, you will find this one to be a little different from those you've used in the past. If this is your first training diary, you probably have a general sense of how to use it but also some questions about which types of information to record and how to record them. In either case, keep reading! You will find the tips you need to get the most out of this tool.

The main body of this training diary consists of preformatted calendar days on which you will write your training (and some nutrition) information. Let's start at the top of each preformatted calendar day and work toward the bottom.

Date. This is left blank so that you can start the diary at any time of the year without wasting pages. The diary has a weekly level of organization (with space for weekly summary information at the end of each), so if you start your diary on a Wednesday, for example, be sure to put your first entry on Wednesday of the first week.

Resting heart rate. Your resting heart rate provides a good indicator of changes in your fitness level and your current level of fatigue. As you gain fitness, your resting heart rate will gradually decrease. When your body is not well-recovered from recent training, your resting heart rate may rise. The best time to measure your resting heart rate is first thing in the morning.

Weight. Many of us weigh ourselves regularly as a way to monitor our health and appearance, but body weight is also a performance-related variable. Your body weight should tend to decrease, if only slightly, as you gain fitness. Getting in the habit of weighing yourself each morning and recording the number will help you stay in touch with this element of your fitness development. Note that your scale weight is affected by your hydration level as well as changes in your actual body mass. So be sure you're adequately hydrated throughout the day.

Distance. Note the total distance of your run. I recommend that you train with a speed and distance device such as a Garmin Forerunner so you can easily record accurate distance information for each of your runs.

Time. Record the total duration of your workout.

Pace/split times. For steady-pace runs, divide the total distance of your run by the total time to determine your average pace for the run. For variable-pace workouts such as interval runs, record your split times for the high-intensity segments (for example, 6 x 400m at 1:49–1:52). Each of your runs should target a particular pace that is appropriate to the specific type of run you're doing and your current fitness level. I recommend that you use my target pace level (TPL) system to determine the right pace for each workout. See Appendix B for an explanation of how to use the TPL system. See Appendix A for a complete menu of running workouts that includes the appropriate pace level(s) to target in each.

Intensity Factor. Intensity Factor is an index that quantifies the overall relative intensity of your run. To calculate it, divide your current "functional threshold pace" in seconds per mile by the average pace of your run in seconds per mile. Your functional threshold pace is your estimate of the fastest pace that you could sustain for 1 hour in race conditions today.

For example, suppose your current estimated functional threshold pace is 6:45 per mile, or 405 seconds per mile. Now suppose your average pace (total time divided by total distance) for today's run is 7:55 per mile, or 475 seconds per mile. This means the Intensity Factor of today's run is 0.85.

Why record this number? Because the intensity of your running is as important as the distance. The distance of a run alone doesn't tell you how hard it was, but the distance and intensity combined do. You will get the best results from your training if you vary the intensity of your runs throughout the week. In a typical week, you should have two runs with Intensity Factors above 0.9 (high intensity), two or three runs with Intensity Factors between 0.7 and 0.8 (low intensity), and the rest between 0.8 and 0.9 (moderate intensity).

Notes. This is a general space to record any other pertinent information about your training. Note whether your workout was a run or another activity, and if it's a run, the specific type of run. (You'll find a menu of basic workout types in Appendix A.)

Describe the weather, first of all. Air temperature and other factors may have a big impact on your running performance on any given day. Recording basic information about the weather during your workouts will put the numbers in context. For example, a slower-than-usual long run in 85-degree heat is not as worrisome as a slower-than-usual long run on a 55-degree day.

Also write down a few words about the course, noting such details as elevation profiles and other factors that affect performance. Include a brief description, such as "San Pablo Dam Loop" or "Washington High Track." Finally, note the shoes you wore so you can keep track of the mileage you put on them. Replace your shoes at least every 500 miles to avoid increasing your injury risk.

For workouts other than runs, record the general information that is most germane to that activity. For example, if you bicycle, note the duration and distance. If you lift weights, note the number of exercises and sets. If you work out twice on any given day (for example, a run in the morning and a strength workout in the afternoon), use the notes space to record the basic details of the second workout. See the sample diary on pages 16–19 for an example of what this looks like.

Aches/pains. Overuse injuries are the bugbear of the runner's life. The primary cause of most running injuries is doing too much too soon. If you respond quickly to signs that an injury is emerging by temporarily reducing your training and then cautiously resuming your ramp-up, you will avoid most breakdowns. Recording the aches and pains you feel in each run will help you catch incipient injuries early.

Rating. Objective workout information is indispensable, but giving each run a general subjective rating is also valuable. Too many "poor" ratings may indicate that you are overtrained, whereas a predominance of "good" and "very good" ratings suggests your training is right on track.

Nutrition. As you know, diet is as important as training with respect to running performance. This section gives you a quick and easy way to monitor the overall quality of your diet. Simply record the number of times you eat foods within each category over the course of the day. Don't get too hung up on portion sizes, although if you eat a very large portion of a certain food you can count it twice, and if you eat a very small portion you can count it as one-half of a full portion.

Aim to consume at least three vegetables and three fruits each day and preferably no fried foods and no more than one sweet. The other categories may vary according to your preferences.

Weekly summary. Record your total running mileage and total training time (including crosstraining sessions) here as well as a line or two about your progress, performance, challenges, and/or any setbacks experienced during the week.

At the end of each week, record your average Intensity Factor for the week. (Add up your Intensity Factors for all the runs you did that week and divide by the number of runs you did.) This will allow you to compare your training from week to week in terms of intensity and not just running distance.

Take a look at a week of my training on pages 16–19.

[2] How to Plan Your Training

If you don't know where you're going, any road will take you there." This expression applies to running as well as it does to anything else. Keeping a training diary is a way of recording where you've been, which will benefit your running in all the ways mentioned in the Introduction to this training diary. But logging alone is not sufficient to guarantee optimal progress in your running. Planning your training is equally important.

Indeed, planning and logging your training are two essential parts of an overarching process that I call "performance management." First you create a sensible training plan that takes you to your next big goal. Then you record the training that you actually do day by day. Finally, you analyze the training you've done and use your observations to make a new and better plan to take you to your next big goal.

This training diary has two distinct spaces for planning. The first is a blank long-term planning calendar on pages 22–25. Use this space for general, long-term planning leading up to your next peak race. Plot all your planned races here, as well as planned weekly mileage totals. The second space for planning is a blank four-week calendar at the beginning of each four-week section of the training diary itself. Use this space for more detailed short-term planning. (See my sample completed four-week planning calendar on pages 20–21.) I recommend that you perform detailed planning in four-week blocks only because it is hard to predict how your body will respond to the training you do over the long term, and your future training should be based on how your body has responded to recent past training.

There are seven steps in the planning process. Let's take a quick look at each of them.

1. SELECT PEAK RACES

The destination of every training plan is a peak race—a race that you wish to run at peak fitness. Although you can have a dozen or more good races in a year, you can't have more than two or three peak races. That's because peak fitness takes a while to build, lasts only a short time, and must be followed by a period of rest and regeneration.

Because of their especially great training demands, peak marathons should be separated by at least 24 weeks. Your second peak race of the year can come as little as 12 weeks after the first if it's a half-marathon or shorter. The same guideline applies to your third peak race—if you wish to squeeze one in. After your last peak race of the year, allow 24 weeks to rest, regenerate, and build toward your first peak race of the next year, regardless of its distance.

You don't have to choose all of your peak races for the coming year at one time. You may choose only your next peak race, if you prefer. Go ahead and note your peak race(s) in the 12-month planning calendar on pages 22–25.

2. SCHEDULE TUNE-UP RACES

It's a good idea to schedule at least one tune-up race before each peak race. Tune-up races are, first of all, great workouts because you always run harder in races than in regular workouts. They also keep you in touch with your capacity to suffer, which you'll need in full measure in your peak race. In addition, tune-up races provide an excellent indication of your fitness level at intermediate points on the way toward a peak and, not least, provide opportunities to pay off all the hard work you do in training.

Don't do too many tune-up races, or your training and/or recovery will suffer. Use common sense in choosing the number and the timing of tune-up races you plan. As a general rule, your tune-up races should be no longer than your peak race, and shorter if your peak race is a marathon.

3. DESIGN A WEEKLY TRAINING CYCLE

Before you can begin to fill in your calendar with workouts, you need to create a weekly training cycle template to use generally in your training. To do this, decide how many times per week you wish to run in the typical week and on which days you will typically perform your long run, high-intensity runs, and base/recovery runs. I recommend that you include one long run and two high-intensity runs in your weekly cycle. Any additional runs should be base/recovery runs. Be sure to include any regular crosstraining that you plan to do in your weekly template as well. I recommend that all runners perform two or three short strength workouts per week. These sessions can be very short (15–20 minutes) and need not take a lot out of you or leave you fatigued for your runs. Separate your strength workouts by at least two days. Otherwise, just fit them into your week at the times that work best for you. Here are suggested templates for 4-, 5-, 6-, and 7-days-a-week runners.

4 Runs Weekly

Mon.	Tues.	Wed.	Thurs.	Fri.	Sat.	Sun.
	High-intensity		Base/Recovery	High-intensity		Long

5 Runs Weekly

Mon.	Tues.	Wed.	Thurs.	Fri.	Sat.	Sun.
	High-intensity		Base/Recovery	High-intensity	Base/Recovery	Long

6 Runs Weekly

Mon.	Tues.	Wed.	Thurs.	Fri.	Sat.	Sun.
	High-intensity	Base/Recovery	Base/Recovery	High-intensity	Base/Recovery	Long

7 Runs Weekly

Mon.	Tues.	Wed.	Thurs.	Fri.	Sat.	Sun.
Base/Recovery	High-intensity	Base/Recovery	Base/Recovery	High-intensity	Base/Recovery	Long

If you wish, you may also include a target Intensity Factor in your weekly workout template. Average Intensity Factors for the workout categories are as follows:

Recovery run	0.70
Base run	0.80
Long run	0.80
High-intensity run	0.92

For more detailed information about Intensity Factors associated with specific workout types, see Appendix A.

4. PLAN PEAK TRAINING WEEKS

The most important week in your training plan is your peak training week, or the week with your heaviest training load, which in most cases should be the second-to-last week before your peak race. This week should include two or three very challenging workouts that put the finishing touches on your race fitness and demonstrate that you are capable of achieving your race goal (assuming you perform as well as expected in these workouts).

Planning this week first—before you plan your preceding training weeks—is helpful because it shows where your training has to go. After this week has been laid out, planning the rest of your training is simply a matter of building your training load step by step from a level that's appropriate to your current fitness level to the level of your peak training week. Following are examples of peak training weeks for 5K, 10K, half-marathon, and marathon peak races.

5K Peak Training Week

Mon.	Tues.	Wed.
Off	**Mixed intervals** 1-mile warm-up 1 mile @ 10K pace (1-min. jog recovery) 2 x 1K @ 5K pace (1-min. jog recoveries) 2 x 600m @ 3K pace (1-min. jog recoveries) 1 x 300m @ 1500m pace 1-mile cool-down	6 miles easy

10K Peak Training Week

Off	**Mixed intervals** 1-mile warm-up 1 x 2K @ half-marathon pace (1-min. jog recovery) 1 mile @ 10K pace (1-min. jog recovery) 2 x 1K @ 5K pace (1-min. jog recoveries) 2 x 800m @ 3K pace (1-min. jog recoveries) 1-mile cool-down	6 miles easy

Half-Marathon Peak Training Week

Off	**Mixed intervals** 1-mile warm-up 2 x 2K @ half-marathon pace (1-min. jog recoveries) 1 mile @ 10K pace (1-min. jog recovery) 1K @ 5K pace (1-min. jog recovery) 800m @ 3K pace (1-min. jog recovery) 1-mile cool-down	6 miles easy

Marathon Peak Training Week

Off	**Mixed intervals** 1-mile warm-up 3K @ half-marathon pace (1-min. jog recovery) 2K @ 10K pace (1-min. jog recovery) 1K @ 5K pace (1-min. jog recovery) 800m @ 3K pace (1-min. jog recovery) 1-mile cool-down	6 miles easy

The time between your peak training week and your peak race is a tapering period, when you reduce your training to promote recovery and race-readiness. Taper one week before 5K and 10K peak races and two weeks before half-marathons and marathons. Cut your peak weekly running mileage by 50 percent in a one-week taper. In a two-week taper, cut your weekly mileage by 50 percent in the first week and by 50 percent again in the second week.

Thurs.	Fri.	Sat.	Sun.
6 miles easy	**1K intervals @ 5K pace** 1-mile warm-up 5 x 1K @ 5K pace (90-sec. jog recoveries) 1-mile cool-down	6 miles easy	**Tempo run** 2 miles easy 4 miles @ 10K pace 2 miles easy
6 miles easy	**3K intervals @ 10K pace** 1.5-mile warm-up 3 x 3K @ 10K pace (90-sec. jog recoveries) 1.5-mile cool-down	6 miles easy	**Tempo run** 2 miles easy 6 miles @ half-marathon pace 2 miles easy
6 miles easy	**Tempo run** 2 miles easy 6 miles @ half-marathon pace 2 miles easy	6 miles easy	**Marathon-pace run** 2-mile warm-up 8 miles @ marathon pace 2-mile cool-down
6 miles easy	**Tempo run** 2 miles easy 8.5 miles @ half-marathon pace 2 miles easy	6 miles easy	**Marathon-pace run** 2-mile warm-up 12 miles @ marathon pace 2-mile cool-down

5. PLAN MILEAGE TARGETS

Add up the total number of miles in your peak training week. This number represents your maximum weekly mileage for your next training cycle. Your first week of training should include roughly the same number of miles as your current training, plus as much as 10 percent. In subsequent weeks, your mileage should gradually increase (by no more than 10 percent per week) until it reaches the designated maximum level.

If you want to be in the best shape possible for your peak race, your weekly mileage should approach maximal level several weeks before your peak training week and then remain relatively steady as you focus on increasing the amount of high-intensity running you do. If your peak race goal is less aggressive, it's okay if your mileage does not reach the peak level until your peak training week.

Don't plan to increase your mileage every single week. Every third or fourth week, reduce your mileage by 20–30 percent to facilitate recovery. Also plan to reduce your mileage in any week that ends with a race.

6. PLAN KEY WORKOUT PROGRESSIONS

Your two weekly high-intensity runs and your weekly long run are your "key workouts"—the workouts that do the most to increase your fitness. As such, they are your most important runs. The next step in the planning process after setting weekly mileage targets is to sketch out the week-by-week development of your key workouts.

The specific types of runs you do as key workouts, the order in which they occur, and their challenge level will depend on the distance of your peak race, the duration of your training cycle, and your fitness level. Refer to Appendix A for a description of the different workouts.

It is beyond the scope of this diary to provide comprehensive guidelines for key workout progressions. But here's a sample 12-week progression of key workouts for a 10K peak race that will give you a general sense of how to do it. (Shaded rows represent recovery weeks.)

Week	High-Intensity Run No. 1	High-Intensity Run No. 2	Long Run
1	*Fartlek Run* 5 miles easy w/ 6 x 30 sec. @ 3K pace	*Progression Run* 4 miles easy + 1 mile @ half-marathon pace	*Long Run* 6 miles easy
2	Fartlek Run 5 miles easy w/ 8 x 30 sec. @ 3K pace	Progression Run 4 miles easy + 1.5 miles @ half-marathon pace	Long Run 7 miles easy
3	*Fartlek Run* 6 miles easy w/ 10 x 30 sec. @ 3K pace	*Progression Run* 4.5 miles easy + 1.5 miles @ half-marathon pace	*Long Run* 8 miles easy
4	*Hill Repetitions* 1-mile warm-up 6 x 400m uphill @ 1500m effort (400m jog recoveries) 1-mile cool-down	*Threshold Run* 1-mile warm-up 2 miles @ half-marathon pace 1-mile cool-down	*Base Run* 6 miles easy
5	*Speed Intervals* 1-mile warm-up 8 x 400m @ 1500m effort (400m jog recoveries) 1-mile cool-down	*Threshold Run* 1-mile warm-up 3 miles @ half-marathon pace 1-mile cool-down	*Progression Run* 7 miles easy + 1 mile @ marathon pace
6	*Hill Repetitions* 1-mile warm-up 10 x 400m uphill @ 1500m effort (400m jog recoveries) 1-mile cool-down	*Threshold Run* 1-mile warm-up 4 miles @ half-marathon pace 1-mile cool-down	*Long Run* 9 miles easy
7	*Speed Intervals* 1-mile warm-up 12 x 400m @ 1500m effort (400m jog recoveries) 1-mile cool-down	*Threshold Run* 1-mile warm-up 2 miles @ half-marathon pace 1 mile easy 2 miles @ 10K pace 1-mile cool-down	*Progression Run* 7 miles easy + 2 miles @ marathon pace
8	*Progression Run* 4 miles easy + 2 miles @ half-marathon pace	*1K Intervals @ 10K Pace* 1-mile warm-up 5 x 1K @ 10K pace (400m jog recoveries) 1-mile cool-down	*Base Run* 6 miles easy
9	*800m Intervals @ 5K Pace* 1-mile warm-up 6 x 800m @ 5K pace (400m active recoveries) 1-mile cool-down	*1-Mile Intervals @ 10K Pace* 1-mile warm-up 5 x 1 mile @ 10K pace (400m jog recoveries) 1-mile cool-down	*Progression Run* 8 miles easy + 2 miles @ half-marathon pace

CONTINUES

Week	High-Intensity Run No. 1	High-Intensity Run No. 2	Long Run
10	*Mixed Intervals* 1-mile warm-up 1 mile @ 10K pace (1-min. jog recovery) 2 x 1K @ 5K pace (1-min. jog recoveries) 2 x 600m @ 3K pace (1-min. jog recovery) 1 x 300m @ 1500m pace 1-mile cool-down	*1-Mile Intervals @ 10K Pace* 1-mile warm-up 6 x 1 mile @ 10K pace (400m jog recoveries) 1-mile cool-down	*Long Run* 12 miles easy
11	*800m Intervals @ 5K Pace* 1-mile warm-up 6 x 800m @ 5K pace (400m active recoveries) 1-mile cool-down	*2K Intervals @ 10K Pace* 1-mile warm-up 5 x 2K @ 10K pace (400m jog recoveries) 1-mile cool-down	*Progression Run* 10 miles easy + 2 miles @ half-marathon pace
12	*Mixed Intervals* 1-mile warm-up 1 mile @ 10K pace (1-min. jog recovery) 1 x 1K @ 5K pace (1-min, jog recoveries) 1 x 600m @ 3K pace (1-min. jog recovery) 1 x 300m @ 1500m pace 1-mile cool-down	*Threshold Run* 1-mile warm-up 2 miles @ 10K pace 1-mile cool-down	**10K Race**

7. FILL IN THE SCHEDULE

The final step of the planning process is to fill in your calendar with base runs and recovery runs. To do so, subtract the combined mileage of your three key workouts from your total planned miles for each week. Distribute the remaining miles among the other days on which you plan to run. Again, it is not necessary to plan every workout in detail all the way from now until your next race. Instead, use the long-term planning calendar on pages 22–25 to plan the general outlines of your training for this period (peak race and tune-up races, weekly mileage targets, weekly workout template), and use the four-week short-term planning calendars that you'll find throughout the diary for more detailed planning (key workout progressions and specific base and recovery runs). You can see a sample of the short-term planning calendar on pages 20–21.

[3] An Experiment of One

Now for a quick peek inside my own "experiment of one" as a runner: First, a week taken from my own training diary. Next, a look what I planned for the four weeks following that week of training. It's my hope that these samples will give you a concrete idea of how to use this diary in your own ongoing experiment of one.

When you glance over the sample diary pages, two things will probably stand out. The first is that I battled a sore hip flexor throughout most of the week. The second is that I did not have many "great" or "very good" workouts. It is seldom possible to develop meaningful hypotheses or conclusions based on a single week's training data, but in the context of continuous training data collection, the two salient aspects of this training week did reinforce a couple of lessons that I have been able to apply since then.

As you see, my hip flexor pain resolved itself by the end of the week without any modification to my planned training. Some aches and pains do that. It so happens that hip flexor pain comes and goes repeatedly as I train. It never develops into a full-blown injury that requires me to stop running, nor do any of my efforts to manage it—mainly stretching and strength training—knock it out for good. It is one of those small bodily nuisances that I can (and must) train through. But other aches and pains behave differently, developing inexorably into debilitating overuse injuries unless you scale back your running. Your training diary can help you distinguish the two types of aches and pains and thereby avoid unnecessary injury setbacks *and* unnecessary training reductions.

As for my subjective workout ratings, I have found that it is normal during periods of intensive training to experience weeks in which I have few "great" or "very good" runs. Only when I go through a week or more without a single "great" or "very good" run do I begin to worry that I might be overtraining and therefore scale back to stimulate recovery.

As a whole, this sample training week indicates that my training was successful and on-track. So the next four weeks of planning represent a continued progression. The only difference is a slight increase in the training load from week to week. As the saying goes, "If it ain't broke, don't fix it."

MONDAY   6/8/09   RESTING HEART RATE   52   WEIGHT   160

DISTANCE 5 mi.   TIME 38:51   PACE/SPLITS 7:46   INTENSITY FACTOR   0.75

Notes Recovery run. Ran office loop . 72° F and dry. Wore Nike Frees.
Strength training 20 min.: dumbbell lunge (2 x 10, 35 lbs.),
side bridge (2 x 30 sec.), push-up (2 x 20), suitcase deadlift (2 x 10, 35 lbs.),
lying draw-in w/ hip flexion (12 reps.)

ACHES AND PAINS Right hip flexor sore.

Rating	GREAT	VERY GOOD	GOOD	✔ FAIR	POOR	VERY BAD

Nutrition	VEGGIE	FRUIT	GRAIN	MEAT/ FISH	NUT/SEED/ BEAN	WATER	SWEET	FRIED
	4	3	4	1		7	2	1

TUESDAY   6/9/09   RESTING HEART RATE   52   WEIGHT   160

DISTANCE 6.25 mi.   TIME 42:40   PACE/SPLITS 6:49   INTENSITY FACTOR   0.86

Notes Lactate intervals at track, 6 x 800m @ 2:34-2:37 with 400m
jog recoveries. 69° F and breezy. Wore racing flats.

ACHES AND PAINS Right hip flexor worse.

Rating	GREAT	VERY GOOD	✔ GOOD	FAIR	POOR	VERY BAD

Nutrition	VEGGIE	FRUIT	GRAIN	MEAT/ FISH	NUT/SEED/ BEAN	WATER	SWEET	FRIED
	3	4	3	2	1	7	1	1

WEDNESDAY   _6/10/09_   RESTING HEART RATE   _53_   WEIGHT   _161_

DISTANCE _5 mi._   TIME _36:00_   PACE/SPLITS _7:12_   INTENSITY FACTOR _0.81_

Notes _Progression run: 4 miles easy + 1 mile @ 6:01. Felt sluggish. 70° F and_
sunny. Wore Nike frees. Office loop. Strength training 20 min.: barbell half-squat
(2 x 8, 185 lbs.), prone plank (2 x 30 sec.), wood chop (2 x 12, 70 lbs.),
reverse wood chop (2 x 12, 90 lbs.), bent-over row (2 x 10, 50 lbs.)

ACHES AND PAINS _Right hip flexor still sore._

Rating	GREAT	VERY GOOD	GOOD	✓ FAIR	POOR	VERY BAD

Nutrition	VEGGIE	FRUIT	GRAIN	MEAT/FISH	NUT/SEED/BEAN	WATER	SWEET	FRIED
	3	3	5	1	0	6	1	1

THURSDAY   _6/11/09_   RESTING HEART RATE   _51_   WEIGHT   _160_

DISTANCE _8.2 mi._   TIME _52:12_   PACE/SPLITS _6:22_   INTENSITY FACTOR _0.92_

Notes _Tempo run on track: 10K @ 36:32._
Felt aerobically easy but legs heavy. 73° F and humid.
Wore racing flats.

ACHES AND PAINS _Hip flexor still sore, right Achilles grumbling a bit._

Rating	GREAT	VERY GOOD	GOOD	✓ FAIR	POOR	VERY BAD

Nutrition	VEGGIE	FRUIT	GRAIN	MEAT/FISH	NUT/SEED/BEAN	WATER	SWEET	FRIED
	4	2	4	2	1	5	2	0

FRIDAY   *6/12/09*   RESTING HEART RATE   *52*   WEIGHT   *161*

DISTANCE *6 mi.*   TIME *45:20*   PACE/SPLITS *7:33*   INTENSITY FACTOR   *0.77*

Notes *Recovery run on office loop. 69° F. Wore Nike frees.*
Strength training 20 min.: split squat jump (2 x 12), push-up (2 x 20),
cable trunk twist (2 x 12, 30 lbs.), single-leg box jump (2 x 12),
chin-up (2 x 10).

ACHES AND PAINS *Right hip flexor nagging.*

Rating	GREAT	VERY GOOD	GOOD	✓ FAIR	POOR	VERY BAD

Nutrition	VEGGIE	FRUIT	GRAIN	MEAT/FISH	NUT/SEED/BEAN	WATER	SWEET	FRIED
	3	3	3	1	1	6	2	1

SATURDAY   *6/13/09*   RESTING HEART RATE   *50*   WEIGHT   *160*

DISTANCE *16 mi.*   TIME *1:55:21*   PACE/SPLITS *7:23*   INTENSITY FACTOR   *0.81*

Notes *Long run, Harbor Island loop. Felt great despite heat!*
Wore Nike Frees. Drank 24 oz. Accelerade.

ACHES AND PAINS *Hip flexor better, left knee a bit sore.*

Rating	✓ GREAT	VERY GOOD	GOOD	FAIR	POOR	VERY BAD

Nutrition	VEGGIE	FRUIT	GRAIN	MEAT/FISH	NUT/SEED/BEAN	WATER	SWEET	FRIED
	4	2	4	2	0	5	2	0

SUNDAY   6/14/09   RESTING HEART RATE 52   WEIGHT 159

DISTANCE 6 mi.   TIME 47:37   PACE/SPLITS 7:56   INTENSITY FACTOR 0.74

Notes _Recovery run on treadmill. Felt good. Wore Nike frees._

ACHES AND PAINS _Hip flexor better._

Rating	GREAT	VERY GOOD	✓ GOOD	FAIR	POOR	VERY BAD

Nutrition	VEGGIE	FRUIT	GRAIN	MEAT/FISH	NUT/SEED/BEAN	WATER	SWEET	FRIED
	3	2	5	2	0	5	2	0

WEEKLY SUMMARY   AVERAGE INTENSITY FACTOR 0.81

	WEEKLY TOTAL	YEAR TO DATE
RUN DISTANCE	52.45 mi.	988 mi.
RUN TIME	4:58:21	123.5 hr.
OTHER TRAINING	1:00	42 hr.
TOTAL TIME	5:58:21	165.5 hr.

Notes _still feeling sluggish on recovery days but stronger and stronger in key workouts._

19

MONDAY	TUESDAY	WEDNESDAY	THURSDAY
6/16	**6/17**	**6/18**	**6/19**
EZ run 6 mi. Strength	800m intervals 8 mi.	EZ run 5 mi. Strength	Progression run 5/1 6 mi. total
6/23	**6/24**	**6/25**	**6/26**
EZ run 6 mi. Strength	1K intervals 8.5 mi.	EZ run 5 mi. Strength	Progression run 5/1.5 6.5 mi. total
6/30	**7/1**	**7/2**	**7/3**
EZ run 7 mi.	1K intervals 9 mi.	EZ run 6 mi. Strength	Fartlek run 7 mi.
7/7	**7/8**	**7/9**	**7/10**
Rest	800m intervals 7 mi.	EZ run 5 mi. Strength	Progression run 4/1 5 mi. total

FRIDAY	SATURDAY	SUNDAY	
6/20	**6/21**	**6/22**	
Threshold run 1/5/1 7 mi. total	EZ run 6 mi.	Long run 11 mi.	**50 mi.** TOTAL DISTANCE
6/27	**6/28**	**6/29**	
Threshold run 1/5.5/1 7.5 mi. total	EZ run 7 mi.	Long run 16 mi.	**56.5 mi.** TOTAL DISTANCE
7/4	**7/5**	**7/6**	
15K race as workout 12 mi. total	EZ run 8 mi.	Long run 17 mi.	**66.5 mi.** TOTAL DISTANCE
7/11	**7/12**	**7/13**	
Threshold run 1/4/1 6 mi. total	EZ run 6 mi.	Long run 13 mi.	**42 mi.** TOTAL DISTANCE

Long-Term Planning Calendar

Use this space to plan your future training with the guidelines presented in the preceding section.

Week of	Mon.	Tues.	Wed.	Thurs.	Fri.	Sat.	Sun.	Weekly Miles

Week of	Mon.	Tues.	Wed.	Thurs.	Fri.	Sat.	Sun.	Weekly Miles

LONG-TERM PLANNING CALENDAR

CONTINUES

Week of	Mon.	Tues.	Wed.	Thurs.	Fri.	Sat.	Sun.	Weekly Miles

Week of	Mon.	Tues.	Wed.	Thurs.	Fri.	Sat.	Sun.	Weekly Miles

MONDAY	TUESDAY	WEDNESDAY	THURSDAY

FRIDAY	SATURDAY	SUNDAY	
			TOTAL DISTANCE
			TOTAL DISTANCE
			TOTAL DISTANCE
			TOTAL DISTANCE

MONDAY ___ / ___ / ___

RESTING HEART RATE _____ WEIGHT _____

DISTANCE _____ TIME _____ PACE/SPLITS _____ INTENSITY FACTOR _____

Notes _____

_____

_____

_____

ACHES AND PAINS _____

Rating	GREAT	VERY GOOD		GOOD	FAIR		POOR	VERY BAD
Nutrition	VEGGIE	FRUIT	GRAIN	MEAT/ FISH	NUT/SEED/ BEAN	WATER	SWEET	FRIED

TUESDAY ___ / ___ / ___

RESTING HEART RATE _____ WEIGHT _____

DISTANCE _____ TIME _____ PACE/SPLITS _____ INTENSITY FACTOR _____

Notes _____

_____

_____

_____

ACHES AND PAINS _____

Rating	GREAT	VERY GOOD		GOOD	FAIR		POOR	VERY BAD
Nutrition	VEGGIE	FRUIT	GRAIN	MEAT/ FISH	NUT/SEED/ BEAN	WATER	SWEET	FRIED

WEDNESDAY ___/___/___   RESTING HEART RATE _____   WEIGHT _____

DISTANCE _____   TIME _____   PACE/SPLITS _____   INTENSITY FACTOR _____

Notes _____

_____

_____

_____

ACHES AND PAINS _____

Rating

| GREAT | VERY GOOD | GOOD | FAIR | POOR | VERY BAD |

Nutrition

| VEGGIE | FRUIT | GRAIN | MEAT/ FISH | NUT/SEED/ BEAN | WATER | SWEET | FRIED |

THURSDAY ___/___/___   RESTING HEART RATE _____   WEIGHT _____

DISTANCE _____   TIME _____   PACE/SPLITS _____   INTENSITY FACTOR _____

Notes _____

_____

_____

_____

ACHES AND PAINS _____

Rating

| GREAT | VERY GOOD | GOOD | FAIR | POOR | VERY BAD |

Nutrition

| VEGGIE | FRUIT | GRAIN | MEAT/ FISH | NUT/SEED/ BEAN | WATER | SWEET | FRIED |

FRIDAY ___ / ___ / ___

RESTING HEART RATE _____ WEIGHT _____

DISTANCE _____ TIME _____ PACE/SPLITS _____ INTENSITY FACTOR _____

Notes _____

_____

_____

_____

_____

ACHES AND PAINS _____

Rating

GREAT	VERY GOOD	GOOD	FAIR	POOR	VERY BAD

Nutrition

VEGGIE	FRUIT	GRAIN	MEAT/ FISH	NUT/SEED/ BEAN	WATER	SWEET	FRIED

SATURDAY ___ / ___ / ___

RESTING HEART RATE _____ WEIGHT _____

DISTANCE _____ TIME _____ PACE/SPLITS _____ INTENSITY FACTOR _____

Notes _____

_____

_____

_____

_____

ACHES AND PAINS _____

Rating

GREAT	VERY GOOD	GOOD	FAIR	POOR	VERY BAD

Nutrition

VEGGIE	FRUIT	GRAIN	MEAT/ FISH	NUT/SEED/ BEAN	WATER	SWEET	FRIED

SUNDAY ___ / ___ / ___

RESTING HEART RATE _____ WEIGHT _____

DISTANCE _____   TIME _____   PACE/SPLITS _____   INTENSITY FACTOR _____

Notes _____

_____

_____

_____

_____

ACHES AND PAINS _____

Rating	GREAT	VERY GOOD		GOOD		FAIR	POOR		VERY BAD
Nutrition	VEGGIE	FRUIT	GRAIN	MEAT/ FISH	NUT/SEED/ BEAN	WATER	SWEET	FRIED	

WEEKLY SUMMARY

AVERAGE INTENSITY FACTOR _____

	WEEKLY TOTAL	YEAR TO DATE
RUN DISTANCE		
RUN TIME		
OTHER TRAINING		
TOTAL TIME		

Notes _____

_____

_____

_____

_____

MONDAY ___ / ___ / ___   RESTING HEART RATE _____ WEIGHT _____

DISTANCE _____   TIME _____   PACE/SPLITS _____   INTENSITY FACTOR _____

Notes _____

_____

_____

_____

ACHES AND PAINS _____

Rating	GREAT	VERY GOOD	GOOD	FAIR	POOR	VERY BAD

Nutrition	VEGGIE	FRUIT	GRAIN	MEAT/FISH	NUT/SEED/BEAN	WATER	SWEET	FRIED

TUESDAY ___ / ___ / ___   RESTING HEART RATE _____ WEIGHT _____

DISTANCE _____   TIME _____   PACE/SPLITS _____   INTENSITY FACTOR _____

Notes _____

_____

_____

_____

ACHES AND PAINS _____

Rating	GREAT	VERY GOOD	GOOD	FAIR	POOR	VERY BAD

Nutrition	VEGGIE	FRUIT	GRAIN	MEAT/FISH	NUT/SEED/BEAN	WATER	SWEET	FRIED

34

WEDNESDAY ___/___/___   RESTING HEART RATE _____   WEIGHT _____

DISTANCE _____   TIME _____   PACE/SPLITS _____   INTENSITY FACTOR _____

Notes _____

_____

_____

_____

ACHES AND PAINS _____

Rating	GREAT	VERY GOOD	GOOD	FAIR	POOR	VERY BAD

Nutrition	VEGGIE	FRUIT	GRAIN	MEAT/ FISH	NUT/SEED/ BEAN	WATER	SWEET	FRIED

THURSDAY ___/___/___   RESTING HEART RATE _____   WEIGHT _____

DISTANCE _____   TIME _____   PACE/SPLITS _____   INTENSITY FACTOR _____

Notes _____

_____

_____

_____

ACHES AND PAINS _____

Rating	GREAT	VERY GOOD	GOOD	FAIR	POOR	VERY BAD

Nutrition	VEGGIE	FRUIT	GRAIN	MEAT/ FISH	NUT/SEED/ BEAN	WATER	SWEET	FRIED

FRIDAY ___ / ___ / ___

RESTING HEART RATE _____ WEIGHT _____

DISTANCE _____ TIME _____ PACE/SPLITS _____ INTENSITY FACTOR _____

Notes _____

_____

_____

_____

_____

ACHES AND PAINS _____

Rating

| GREAT | VERY GOOD | GOOD | FAIR | POOR | VERY BAD |

Nutrition

VEGGIE	FRUIT	GRAIN	MEAT/ FISH	NUT/SEED/ BEAN	WATER	SWEET	FRIED

SATURDAY ___ / ___ / ___

RESTING HEART RATE _____ WEIGHT _____

DISTANCE _____ TIME _____ PACE/SPLITS _____ INTENSITY FACTOR _____

Notes _____

_____

_____

_____

_____

ACHES AND PAINS _____

Rating

| GREAT | VERY GOOD | GOOD | FAIR | POOR | VERY BAD |

Nutrition

VEGGIE	FRUIT	GRAIN	MEAT/ FISH	NUT/SEED/ BEAN	WATER	SWEET	FRIED

SUNDAY ___ / ___ / ___

RESTING HEART RATE _____ WEIGHT _____

DISTANCE _____ TIME _____ PACE/SPLITS _____ INTENSITY FACTOR _____

Notes _____

_____

_____

_____

_____

_____

ACHES AND PAINS _____

Rating

| GREAT | VERY GOOD | GOOD | FAIR | POOR | VERY BAD |

Nutrition

| VEGGIE | FRUIT | GRAIN | MEAT/ FISH | NUT/SEED/ BEAN | WATER | SWEET | FRIED |

WEEKLY SUMMARY

AVERAGE INTENSITY FACTOR _____

	WEEKLY TOTAL	YEAR TO DATE
RUN DISTANCE		
RUN TIME		
OTHER TRAINING		
TOTAL TIME		

Notes _____

_____

_____

_____

_____

MONDAY ___ / ___ / ___   RESTING HEART RATE _____ WEIGHT _____

DISTANCE _____   TIME _____   PACE/SPLITS _____   INTENSITY FACTOR _____

Notes _____

_____

_____

_____

ACHES AND PAINS _____

Rating	GREAT	VERY GOOD	GOOD	FAIR	POOR	VERY BAD

Nutrition	VEGGIE	FRUIT	GRAIN	MEAT/ FISH	NUT/SEED/ BEAN	WATER	SWEET	FRIED

TUESDAY ___ / ___ / ___   RESTING HEART RATE _____ WEIGHT _____

DISTANCE _____   TIME _____   PACE/SPLITS _____   INTENSITY FACTOR _____

Notes _____

_____

_____

_____

ACHES AND PAINS _____

Rating	GREAT	VERY GOOD	GOOD	FAIR	POOR	VERY BAD

Nutrition	VEGGIE	FRUIT	GRAIN	MEAT/ FISH	NUT/SEED/ BEAN	WATER	SWEET	FRIED

WEDNESDAY ___ / ___ / ___   RESTING HEART RATE _____ WEIGHT _____

DISTANCE _____   TIME _____   PACE/SPLITS _____   INTENSITY FACTOR _____

Notes _____
_____
_____
_____

ACHES AND PAINS _____

Rating	GREAT	VERY GOOD		GOOD	FAIR	POOR	VERY BAD
Nutrition	VEGGIE	FRUIT	GRAIN	MEAT/ FISH	NUT/SEED/ BEAN	WATER	SWEET	FRIED

THURSDAY ___ / ___ / ___   RESTING HEART RATE _____ WEIGHT _____

DISTANCE _____   TIME _____   PACE/SPLITS _____   INTENSITY FACTOR _____

Notes _____
_____
_____
_____

ACHES AND PAINS _____

Rating	GREAT	VERY GOOD		GOOD	FAIR	POOR	VERY BAD
Nutrition	VEGGIE	FRUIT	GRAIN	MEAT/ FISH	NUT/SEED/ BEAN	WATER	SWEET	FRIED

FRIDAY ___ / ___ / ___

RESTING HEART RATE _____ WEIGHT _____

DISTANCE _____ TIME _____ PACE/SPLITS _____ INTENSITY FACTOR _____

Notes _____

_____

_____

_____

_____

ACHES AND PAINS _____

Rating	GREAT	VERY GOOD	GOOD	FAIR	POOR	VERY BAD

Nutrition	VEGGIE	FRUIT	GRAIN	MEAT/ FISH	NUT/SEED/ BEAN	WATER	SWEET	FRIED

SATURDAY ___ / ___ / ___

RESTING HEART RATE _____ WEIGHT _____

DISTANCE _____ TIME _____ PACE/SPLITS _____ INTENSITY FACTOR _____

Notes _____

_____

_____

_____

_____

ACHES AND PAINS _____

Rating	GREAT	VERY GOOD	GOOD	FAIR	POOR	VERY BAD

Nutrition	VEGGIE	FRUIT	GRAIN	MEAT/ FISH	NUT/SEED/ BEAN	WATER	SWEET	FRIED

SUNDAY ___ / ___ / ___

RESTING HEART RATE _____ WEIGHT _____

DISTANCE _____ TIME _____ PACE/SPLITS _____ INTENSITY FACTOR _____

Notes _____

_____

_____

_____

_____

ACHES AND PAINS _____

Rating	GREAT	VERY GOOD		GOOD	FAIR		POOR		VERY BAD
Nutrition	VEGGIE	FRUIT	GRAIN	MEAT/ FISH	NUT/SEED/ BEAN	WATER	SWEET	FRIED

WEEKLY SUMMARY

AVERAGE INTENSITY FACTOR _____

	WEEKLY TOTAL	YEAR TO DATE
RUN DISTANCE		
RUN TIME		
OTHER TRAINING		
TOTAL TIME		

Notes _____

_____

_____

_____

_____

MONDAY ___ / ___ / ___   RESTING HEART RATE _____ WEIGHT _____

DISTANCE _____   TIME _____   PACE/SPLITS _____   INTENSITY FACTOR _____

Notes _____

_____

_____

_____

ACHES AND PAINS _____

Rating	GREAT	VERY GOOD	GOOD	FAIR	POOR	VERY BAD

Nutrition	VEGGIE	FRUIT	GRAIN	MEAT/FISH	NUT/SEED/BEAN	WATER	SWEET	FRIED

TUESDAY ___ / ___ / ___   RESTING HEART RATE _____ WEIGHT _____

DISTANCE _____   TIME _____   PACE/SPLITS _____   INTENSITY FACTOR _____

Notes _____

_____

_____

_____

ACHES AND PAINS _____

Rating	GREAT	VERY GOOD	GOOD	FAIR	POOR	VERY BAD

Nutrition	VEGGIE	FRUIT	GRAIN	MEAT/FISH	NUT/SEED/BEAN	WATER	SWEET	FRIED

us, you can reduce your injury risk by running in the lightest, least cushioned, and most flexible shoes that are comfortable for you.

WEDNESDAY ___ / ___ / ___   RESTING HEART RATE _____ WEIGHT _____

DISTANCE _____   TIME _____   PACE/SPLITS _____   INTENSITY FACTOR _____

Notes _____

_____

_____

_____

ACHES AND PAINS _____

Rating	GREAT	VERY GOOD		GOOD	FAIR		POOR	VERY BAD
Nutrition	VEGGIE	FRUIT	GRAIN	MEAT/ FISH	NUT/SEED/ BEAN	WATER	SWEET	FRIED

THURSDAY ___ / ___ / ___   RESTING HEART RATE _____ WEIGHT _____

DISTANCE _____   TIME _____   PACE/SPLITS _____   INTENSITY FACTOR _____

Notes _____

_____

_____

_____

ACHES AND PAINS _____

Rating	GREAT	VERY GOOD		GOOD	FAIR		POOR	VERY BAD
Nutrition	VEGGIE	FRUIT	GRAIN	MEAT/ FISH	NUT/SEED/ BEAN	WATER	SWEET	FRIED

FRIDAY ___ / ___ / ___

RESTING HEART RATE _____ WEIGHT _____

DISTANCE _____ TIME _____ PACE/SPLITS _____ INTENSITY FACTOR _____

Notes _____

_____

_____

_____

_____

ACHES AND PAINS _____

Rating	GREAT	VERY GOOD	GOOD	FAIR	POOR	VERY BAD

Nutrition	VEGGIE	FRUIT	GRAIN	MEAT/ FISH	NUT/SEED/ BEAN	WATER	SWEET	FRIED

SATURDAY ___ / ___ / ___

RESTING HEART RATE _____ WEIGHT _____

DISTANCE _____ TIME _____ PACE/SPLITS _____ INTENSITY FACTOR _____

Notes _____

_____

_____

_____

_____

ACHES AND PAINS _____

Rating	GREAT	VERY GOOD	GOOD	FAIR	POOR	VERY BAD

Nutrition	VEGGIE	FRUIT	GRAIN	MEAT/ FISH	NUT/SEED/ BEAN	WATER	SWEET	FRIED

SUNDAY ___ / ___ / ___

RESTING HEART RATE _____ WEIGHT _____

DISTANCE _____ TIME _____ PACE/SPLITS _____ INTENSITY FACTOR _____

Notes _____

_____

_____

_____

_____

_____

ACHES AND PAINS _____

Rating	GREAT	VERY GOOD	GOOD	FAIR	POOR	VERY BAD

Nutrition	VEGGIE	FRUIT	GRAIN	MEAT/FISH	NUT/SEED/BEAN	WATER	SWEET	FRIED

WEEKLY SUMMARY

AVERAGE INTENSITY FACTOR _____

	WEEKLY TOTAL	YEAR TO DATE
RUN DISTANCE		
RUN TIME		
OTHER TRAINING		
TOTAL TIME		

Notes _____

_____

_____

_____

_____

45

MONDAY	TUESDAY	WEDNESDAY	THURSDAY

FRIDAY   SATURDAY   SUNDAY

TOTAL DISTANCE

TOTAL DISTANCE

TOTAL DISTANCE

TOTAL DISTANCE

MONDAY ___ / ___ / ___   RESTING HEART RATE _____ WEIGHT _____

DISTANCE _____   TIME _____   PACE/SPLITS _____   INTENSITY FACTOR _____

Notes _____

_____

_____

_____

ACHES AND PAINS _____

Rating	GREAT	VERY GOOD	GOOD	FAIR	POOR	VERY BAD
Nutrition	VEGGIE	FRUIT	GRAIN	MEAT/FISH	NUT/SEED/BEAN	WATER	SWEET	FRIED

TUESDAY ___ / ___ / ___   RESTING HEART RATE _____ WEIGHT _____

DISTANCE _____   TIME _____   PACE/SPLITS _____   INTENSITY FACTOR _____

Notes _____

_____

_____

_____

ACHES AND PAINS _____

Rating	GREAT	VERY GOOD	GOOD	FAIR	POOR	VERY BAD
Nutrition	VEGGIE	FRUIT	GRAIN	MEAT/FISH	NUT/SEED/BEAN	WATER	SWEET	FRIED

forces and hence the risk of injury. If you're a heel striker, gradually train yourself to shorten your stride.

WEDNESDAY ___ / ___ / ___   RESTING HEART RATE _____   WEIGHT _____

DISTANCE _____   TIME _____   PACE/SPLITS _____   INTENSITY FACTOR _____

Notes _____

_____

_____

_____

ACHES AND PAINS _____

Rating	GREAT	VERY GOOD		GOOD	FAIR		POOR	VERY BAD
Nutrition	VEGGIE	FRUIT	GRAIN	MEAT/ FISH	NUT/SEED/ BEAN	WATER	SWEET	FRIED

THURSDAY ___ / ___ / ___   RESTING HEART RATE _____   WEIGHT _____

DISTANCE _____   TIME _____   PACE/SPLITS _____   INTENSITY FACTOR _____

Notes _____

_____

_____

_____

ACHES AND PAINS _____

Rating	GREAT	VERY GOOD		GOOD	FAIR		POOR	VERY BAD
Nutrition	VEGGIE	FRUIT	GRAIN	MEAT/ FISH	NUT/SEED/ BEAN	WATER	SWEET	FRIED

FRIDAY ___ / ___ / ___

RESTING HEART RATE _____ WEIGHT _____

DISTANCE _____ TIME _____ PACE/SPLITS _____ INTENSITY FACTOR _____

Notes _____

_____

_____

_____

_____

ACHES AND PAINS _____

Rating	GREAT	VERY GOOD		GOOD	FAIR	POOR	VERY BAD
Nutrition	VEGGIE	FRUIT	GRAIN	MEAT/ FISH	NUT/SEED/ BEAN	WATER	SWEET	FRIED

SATURDAY ___ / ___ / ___

RESTING HEART RATE _____ WEIGHT _____

DISTANCE _____ TIME _____ PACE/SPLITS _____ INTENSITY FACTOR _____

Notes _____

_____

_____

_____

_____

ACHES AND PAINS _____

Rating	GREAT	VERY GOOD		GOOD	FAIR	POOR	VERY BAD
Nutrition	VEGGIE	FRUIT	GRAIN	MEAT/ FISH	NUT/SEED/ BEAN	WATER	SWEET	FRIED

SUNDAY ___ / ___ / ___

RESTING HEART RATE _____ WEIGHT _____

DISTANCE _____ TIME _____ PACE/SPLITS _____ INTENSITY FACTOR _____

Notes _____

_____

_____

_____

_____

_____

ACHES AND PAINS _____

Rating

| GREAT | VERY GOOD | GOOD | FAIR | POOR | VERY BAD |

Nutrition

VEGGIE	FRUIT	GRAIN	MEAT/ FISH	NUT/SEED/ BEAN	WATER	SWEET	FRIED

WEEKLY SUMMARY

AVERAGE INTENSITY FACTOR _____

	WEEKLY TOTAL	YEAR TO DATE
RUN DISTANCE		
RUN TIME		
OTHER TRAINING		
TOTAL TIME		

Notes _____

_____

_____

_____

_____

MONDAY ___ / ___ / ___   RESTING HEART RATE _____   WEIGHT _____

DISTANCE _____   TIME _____   PACE/SPLITS _____   INTENSITY FACTOR _____

Notes _____

_____

_____

_____

ACHES AND PAINS _____

Rating	GREAT	VERY GOOD		GOOD	FAIR	POOR		VERY BAD
Nutrition	VEGGIE	FRUIT	GRAIN	MEAT/ FISH	NUT/SEED/ BEAN	WATER	SWEET	FRIED

TUESDAY ___ / ___ / ___   RESTING HEART RATE _____   WEIGHT _____

DISTANCE _____   TIME _____   PACE/SPLITS _____   INTENSITY FACTOR _____

Notes _____

_____

_____

_____

ACHES AND PAINS _____

Rating	GREAT	VERY GOOD		GOOD	FAIR	POOR		VERY BAD
Nutrition	VEGGIE	FRUIT	GRAIN	MEAT/ FISH	NUT/SEED/ BEAN	WATER	SWEET	FRIED

WEDNESDAY ___ / ___ / ___   RESTING HEART RATE _____ WEIGHT _____

DISTANCE _____   TIME _____   PACE/SPLITS _____   INTENSITY FACTOR _____

Notes _____

_____

_____

_____

ACHES AND PAINS _____

Rating   GREAT   VERY GOOD   GOOD   FAIR   POOR   VERY BAD

Nutrition   VEGGIE   FRUIT   GRAIN   MEAT/   NUT/SEED/   WATER   SWEET   FRIED
                                        FISH   BEAN

THURSDAY ___ / ___ / ___   RESTING HEART RATE _____ WEIGHT _____

DISTANCE _____   TIME _____   PACE/SPLITS _____   INTENSITY FACTOR _____

Notes _____

_____

_____

_____

ACHES AND PAINS _____

Rating   GREAT   VERY GOOD   GOOD   FAIR   POOR   VERY BAD

Nutrition   VEGGIE   FRUIT   GRAIN   MEAT/   NUT/SEED/   WATER   SWEET   FRIED
                                        FISH   BEAN

53

FRIDAY ___/___/___

RESTING HEART RATE _____ WEIGHT _____

DISTANCE _____ TIME _____ PACE/SPLITS _____ INTENSITY FACTOR _____

Notes _____

_____

_____

_____

_____

ACHES AND PAINS _____

Rating	GREAT	VERY GOOD		GOOD		FAIR	POOR	VERY BAD
Nutrition	VEGGIE	FRUIT	GRAIN	MEAT/FISH	NUT/SEED/BEAN	WATER	SWEET	FRIED

SATURDAY ___/___/___

RESTING HEART RATE _____ WEIGHT _____

DISTANCE _____ TIME _____ PACE/SPLITS _____ INTENSITY FACTOR _____

Notes _____

_____

_____

_____

_____

ACHES AND PAINS _____

Rating	GREAT	VERY GOOD		GOOD		FAIR	POOR	VERY BAD
Nutrition	VEGGIE	FRUIT	GRAIN	MEAT/FISH	NUT/SEED/BEAN	WATER	SWEET	FRIED

SUNDAY ___ / ___ / ___

RESTING HEART RATE _____ WEIGHT _____

DISTANCE _____ TIME _____ PACE/SPLITS _____ INTENSITY FACTOR _____

Notes _____

_____

_____

_____

_____

_____

ACHES AND PAINS _____

Rating	GREAT	VERY GOOD	GOOD	FAIR	POOR	VERY BAD

Nutrition	VEGGIE	FRUIT	GRAIN	MEAT/ FISH	NUT/SEED/ BEAN	WATER	SWEET	FRIED

WEEKLY SUMMARY

AVERAGE INTENSITY FACTOR _____

	WEEKLY TOTAL	YEAR TO DATE
RUN DISTANCE		
RUN TIME		
OTHER TRAINING		
TOTAL TIME		

Notes _____

_____

_____

_____

_____

MONDAY ____ / ____ / ____   RESTING HEART RATE _____ WEIGHT _____

DISTANCE _____   TIME _____   PACE/SPLITS _____   INTENSITY FACTOR _____

Notes _____
_____
_____
_____

ACHES AND PAINS _____

Rating   GREAT   VERY GOOD   GOOD   FAIR   POOR   VERY BAD

Nutrition   VEGGIE   FRUIT   GRAIN   MEAT/   NUT/SEED/   WATER   SWEET   FRIED
                                          FISH   BEAN

TUESDAY ____ / ____ / ____   RESTING HEART RATE _____ WEIGHT _____

DISTANCE _____   TIME _____   PACE/SPLITS _____   INTENSITY FACTOR _____

Notes _____
_____
_____
_____

ACHES AND PAINS _____

Rating   GREAT   VERY GOOD   GOOD   FAIR   POOR   VERY BAD

Nutrition   VEGGIE   FRUIT   GRAIN   MEAT/   NUT/SEED/   WATER   SWEET   FRIED
                                          FISH   BEAN

as a regular bathroom scale and cost about the same. Step on once a week and look for a gradual downward trend in your body fat percentage.

WEDNESDAY ___ / ___ / ___   RESTING HEART RATE _____ WEIGHT _____

DISTANCE _____   TIME _____   PACE/SPLITS _____   INTENSITY FACTOR _____

Notes _____

_____

_____

_____

ACHES AND PAINS _____

Rating	GREAT	VERY GOOD	GOOD	FAIR	POOR	VERY BAD

Nutrition	VEGGIE	FRUIT	GRAIN	MEAT/FISH	NUT/SEED/BEAN	WATER	SWEET	FRIED

THURSDAY ___ / ___ / ___   RESTING HEART RATE _____ WEIGHT _____

DISTANCE _____   TIME _____   PACE/SPLITS _____   INTENSITY FACTOR _____

Notes _____

_____

_____

_____

ACHES AND PAINS _____

Rating	GREAT	VERY GOOD	GOOD	FAIR	POOR	VERY BAD

Nutrition	VEGGIE	FRUIT	GRAIN	MEAT/FISH	NUT/SEED/BEAN	WATER	SWEET	FRIED

FRIDAY ___ / ___ / ___

RESTING HEART RATE _____ WEIGHT _____

DISTANCE _____ TIME _____ PACE/SPLITS _____ INTENSITY FACTOR _____

Notes _____

_____

_____

_____

_____

ACHES AND PAINS _____

Rating	GREAT		VERY GOOD		GOOD		FAIR		POOR		VERY BAD

Nutrition	VEGGIE	FRUIT	GRAIN	MEAT/ FISH	NUT/SEED/ BEAN	WATER	SWEET	FRIED

SATURDAY ___ / ___ / ___

RESTING HEART RATE _____ WEIGHT _____

DISTANCE _____ TIME _____ PACE/SPLITS _____ INTENSITY FACTOR _____

Notes _____

_____

_____

_____

_____

ACHES AND PAINS _____

Rating	GREAT		VERY GOOD		GOOD		FAIR		POOR		VERY BAD

Nutrition	VEGGIE	FRUIT	GRAIN	MEAT/ FISH	NUT/SEED/ BEAN	WATER	SWEET	FRIED

SUNDAY ___ / ___ / ___

RESTING HEART RATE _____ WEIGHT _____

DISTANCE _____ TIME _____ PACE/SPLITS _____ INTENSITY FACTOR _____

Notes _____

_____

_____

_____

_____

_____

ACHES AND PAINS _____

Rating	GREAT	VERY GOOD	GOOD	FAIR	POOR	VERY BAD

Nutrition	VEGGIE	FRUIT	GRAIN	MEAT/FISH	NUT/SEED/BEAN	WATER	SWEET	FRIED

WEEKLY SUMMARY

AVERAGE INTENSITY FACTOR _____

	WEEKLY TOTAL	YEAR TO DATE
RUN DISTANCE		
RUN TIME		
OTHER TRAINING		
TOTAL TIME		

Notes _____

_____

_____

_____

_____

MONDAY ___ / ___ / ___   RESTING HEART RATE _____ WEIGHT _____

DISTANCE _____   TIME _____   PACE/SPLITS _____   INTENSITY FACTOR _____

Notes _____
_____
_____
_____

ACHES AND PAINS _____

Rating	GREAT	VERY GOOD	GOOD	FAIR	POOR	VERY BAD

Nutrition	VEGGIE	FRUIT	GRAIN	MEAT/FISH	NUT/SEED/BEAN	WATER	SWEET	FRIED

TUESDAY ___ / ___ / ___   RESTING HEART RATE _____ WEIGHT _____

DISTANCE _____   TIME _____   PACE/SPLITS _____   INTENSITY FACTOR _____

Notes _____
_____
_____
_____

ACHES AND PAINS _____

Rating	GREAT	VERY GOOD	GOOD	FAIR	POOR	VERY BAD

Nutrition	VEGGIE	FRUIT	GRAIN	MEAT/FISH	NUT/SEED/BEAN	WATER	SWEET	FRIED

running as you can do pain-free (which might be no running at all for a few days) until the problem is gone.

WEDNESDAY ___ / ___ / ___   RESTING HEART RATE ___   WEIGHT ___

DISTANCE ___   TIME ___   PACE/SPLITS ___   INTENSITY FACTOR ___

Notes ___

___

___

___

ACHES AND PAINS ___

Rating

| GREAT | VERY GOOD | GOOD | FAIR | POOR | VERY BAD |

Nutrition

| VEGGIE | FRUIT | GRAIN | MEAT/ FISH | NUT/SEED/ BEAN | WATER | SWEET | FRIED |

THURSDAY ___ / ___ / ___   RESTING HEART RATE ___   WEIGHT ___

DISTANCE ___   TIME ___   PACE/SPLITS ___   INTENSITY FACTOR ___

Notes ___

___

___

___

ACHES AND PAINS ___

Rating

| GREAT | VERY GOOD | GOOD | FAIR | POOR | VERY BAD |

Nutrition

| VEGGIE | FRUIT | GRAIN | MEAT/ FISH | NUT/SEED/ BEAN | WATER | SWEET | FRIED |

FRIDAY ___/___/___

RESTING HEART RATE _____ WEIGHT _____

DISTANCE _____ TIME _____ PACE/SPLITS _____ INTENSITY FACTOR _____

Notes _____

_____

_____

_____

_____

ACHES AND PAINS _____

Rating	GREAT	VERY GOOD	GOOD	FAIR	POOR	VERY BAD

Nutrition	VEGGIE	FRUIT	GRAIN	MEAT/FISH	NUT/SEED/BEAN	WATER	SWEET	FRIED

SATURDAY ___/___/___

RESTING HEART RATE _____ WEIGHT _____

DISTANCE _____ TIME _____ PACE/SPLITS _____ INTENSITY FACTOR _____

Notes _____

_____

_____

_____

_____

ACHES AND PAINS _____

Rating	GREAT	VERY GOOD	GOOD	FAIR	POOR	VERY BAD

Nutrition	VEGGIE	FRUIT	GRAIN	MEAT/FISH	NUT/SEED/BEAN	WATER	SWEET	FRIED

62

SUNDAY ___ / ___ / ___

RESTING HEART RATE _____ WEIGHT _____

DISTANCE _____ TIME _____ PACE/SPLITS _____ INTENSITY FACTOR _____

Notes _____

_____

_____

_____

_____

_____

ACHES AND PAINS _____

Rating

| GREAT | VERY GOOD | GOOD | FAIR | POOR | VERY BAD |

Nutrition

| VEGGIE | FRUIT | GRAIN | MEAT/ FISH | NUT/SEED/ BEAN | WATER | SWEET | FRIED |

WEEKLY SUMMARY

AVERAGE INTENSITY FACTOR _____

	WEEKLY TOTAL	YEAR TO DATE
RUN DISTANCE		
RUN TIME		
OTHER TRAINING		
TOTAL TIME		

Notes _____

_____

_____

_____

_____

MONDAY	TUESDAY	WEDNESDAY	THURSDAY

TOTAL DISTANCE

TOTAL DISTANCE

TOTAL DISTANCE

TOTAL DISTANCE

PLANNING CALENDAR

MONDAY ___ / ___ / ___   RESTING HEART RATE _____ WEIGHT _____

DISTANCE _____   TIME _____   PACE/SPLITS _____   INTENSITY FACTOR _____

Notes _____

_____

_____

_____

ACHES AND PAINS _____

Rating	GREAT		VERY GOOD		GOOD	FAIR		POOR		VERY BAD
Nutrition	VEGGIE	FRUIT	GRAIN	MEAT/ FISH	NUT/SEED/ BEAN	WATER	SWEET	FRIED		

TUESDAY ___ / ___ / ___   RESTING HEART RATE _____ WEIGHT _____

DISTANCE _____   TIME _____   PACE/SPLITS _____   INTENSITY FACTOR _____

Notes _____

_____

_____

_____

ACHES AND PAINS _____

Rating	GREAT		VERY GOOD		GOOD	FAIR		POOR		VERY BAD
Nutrition	VEGGIE	FRUIT	GRAIN	MEAT/ FISH	NUT/SEED/ BEAN	WATER	SWEET	FRIED		

core by doing a few strengthening exercises such as Swiss ball crunches two or three times a week.

WEDNESDAY ___ / ___ / ___   RESTING HEART RATE _____   WEIGHT _____

DISTANCE _____   TIME _____   PACE/SPLITS _____   INTENSITY FACTOR _____

Notes _____

_____

_____

_____

ACHES AND PAINS _____

Rating	GREAT	VERY GOOD	GOOD	FAIR	POOR	VERY BAD	
Nutrition	VEGGIE	FRUIT	GRAIN	MEAT/FISH	NUT/SEED/BEAN	WATER	SWEET	FRIED

THURSDAY ___ / ___ / ___   RESTING HEART RATE _____   WEIGHT _____

DISTANCE _____   TIME _____   PACE/SPLITS _____   INTENSITY FACTOR _____

Notes _____

_____

_____

_____

ACHES AND PAINS _____

Rating	GREAT	VERY GOOD	GOOD	FAIR	POOR	VERY BAD	
Nutrition	VEGGIE	FRUIT	GRAIN	MEAT/FISH	NUT/SEED/BEAN	WATER	SWEET	FRIED

FRIDAY ____ / ____ / ____

RESTING HEART RATE _____ WEIGHT _____

DISTANCE _____ TIME _____ PACE/SPLITS _____ INTENSITY FACTOR _____

Notes _____

_____

_____

_____

_____

ACHES AND PAINS _____

Rating	GREAT		VERY GOOD		GOOD		FAIR		POOR		VERY BAD

Nutrition	VEGGIE	FRUIT	GRAIN	MEAT/FISH	NUT/SEED/BEAN	WATER	SWEET	FRIED

SATURDAY ____ / ____ / ____

RESTING HEART RATE _____ WEIGHT _____

DISTANCE _____ TIME _____ PACE/SPLITS _____ INTENSITY FACTOR _____

Notes _____

_____

_____

_____

_____

ACHES AND PAINS _____

Rating	GREAT		VERY GOOD		GOOD		FAIR		POOR		VERY BAD

Nutrition	VEGGIE	FRUIT	GRAIN	MEAT/FISH	NUT/SEED/BEAN	WATER	SWEET	FRIED

SUNDAY ___ / ___ / ___

RESTING HEART RATE _____ WEIGHT _____

DISTANCE _____ TIME _____ PACE/SPLITS _____ INTENSITY FACTOR _____

Notes _____

_____

_____

_____

_____

ACHES AND PAINS _____

Rating	GREAT	VERY GOOD	GOOD	FAIR	POOR	VERY BAD

Nutrition	VEGGIE	FRUIT	GRAIN	MEAT/FISH	NUT/SEED/BEAN	WATER	SWEET	FRIED

WEEKLY SUMMARY

AVERAGE INTENSITY FACTOR _____

	WEEKLY TOTAL	YEAR TO DATE
RUN DISTANCE		
RUN TIME		
OTHER TRAINING		
TOTAL TIME		

Notes _____

_____

_____

_____

_____

MONDAY ___ / ___ / ___   RESTING HEART RATE _____ WEIGHT _____

DISTANCE _____   TIME _____   PACE/SPLITS _____   INTENSITY FACTOR _____

Notes _____
_____
_____
_____

ACHES AND PAINS _____

Rating

GREAT	VERY GOOD	GOOD	FAIR	POOR	VERY BAD

Nutrition

VEGGIE	FRUIT	GRAIN	MEAT/ FISH	NUT/SEED/ BEAN	WATER	SWEET	FRIED

TUESDAY ___ / ___ / ___   RESTING HEART RATE _____ WEIGHT _____

DISTANCE _____   TIME _____   PACE/SPLITS _____   INTENSITY FACTOR _____

Notes _____
_____
_____
_____

ACHES AND PAINS _____

Rating

GREAT	VERY GOOD	GOOD	FAIR	POOR	VERY BAD

Nutrition

VEGGIE	FRUIT	GRAIN	MEAT/ FISH	NUT/SEED/ BEAN	WATER	SWEET	FRIED

training for a few days to shake off the excess fatigue and then resume normal training.

WEDNESDAY ____ / ____ / ____   RESTING HEART RATE _____   WEIGHT _____

DISTANCE _____   TIME _____   PACE/SPLITS _____   INTENSITY FACTOR _____

Notes _____

_____

_____

_____

ACHES AND PAINS _____

Rating	GREAT		VERY GOOD		GOOD		FAIR		POOR		VERY BAD
Nutrition	VEGGIE	FRUIT	GRAIN	MEAT/ FISH	NUT/SEED/ BEAN	WATER	SWEET	FRIED			

THURSDAY ____ / ____ / ____   RESTING HEART RATE _____   WEIGHT _____

DISTANCE _____   TIME _____   PACE/SPLITS _____   INTENSITY FACTOR _____

Notes _____

_____

_____

_____

ACHES AND PAINS _____

Rating	GREAT		VERY GOOD		GOOD		FAIR		POOR		VERY BAD
Nutrition	VEGGIE	FRUIT	GRAIN	MEAT/ FISH	NUT/SEED/ BEAN	WATER	SWEET	FRIED			

FRIDAY ___ / ___ / ___

RESTING HEART RATE _____ WEIGHT _____

DISTANCE _____ TIME _____ PACE/SPLITS _____ INTENSITY FACTOR _____

Notes _____
_____
_____
_____
_____

ACHES AND PAINS _____

Rating	GREAT	VERY GOOD	GOOD	FAIR	POOR	VERY BAD

Nutrition	VEGGIE	FRUIT	GRAIN	MEAT/ FISH	NUT/SEED/ BEAN	WATER	SWEET	FRIED

SATURDAY ___ / ___ / ___

RESTING HEART RATE _____ WEIGHT _____

DISTANCE _____ TIME _____ PACE/SPLITS _____ INTENSITY FACTOR _____

Notes _____
_____
_____
_____
_____

ACHES AND PAINS _____

Rating	GREAT	VERY GOOD	GOOD	FAIR	POOR	VERY BAD

Nutrition	VEGGIE	FRUIT	GRAIN	MEAT/ FISH	NUT/SEED/ BEAN	WATER	SWEET	FRIED

SUNDAY ___ / ___ / ___   RESTING HEART RATE _____   WEIGHT _____

DISTANCE _____   TIME _____   PACE/SPLITS _____   INTENSITY FACTOR _____

Notes _____

_____

_____

_____

_____

_____

ACHES AND PAINS _____

Rating

GREAT	VERY GOOD	GOOD	FAIR	POOR	VERY BAD

Nutrition

VEGGIE	FRUIT	GRAIN	MEAT/ FISH	NUT/SEED/ BEAN	WATER	SWEET	FRIED

WEEKLY SUMMARY   AVERAGE INTENSITY FACTOR _____

	WEEKLY TOTAL	YEAR TO DATE
RUN DISTANCE		
RUN TIME		
OTHER TRAINING		
TOTAL TIME		

Notes _____

_____

_____

_____

_____

MONDAY ___ / ___ / ___   RESTING HEART RATE _____ WEIGHT _____

DISTANCE _____   TIME _____   PACE/SPLITS _____   INTENSITY FACTOR _____

Notes _____

_____

_____

_____

ACHES AND PAINS _____

Rating	GREAT	VERY GOOD		GOOD	FAIR		POOR	VERY BAD
Nutrition	VEGGIE	FRUIT	GRAIN	MEAT/ FISH	NUT/SEED/ BEAN	WATER	SWEET	FRIED

TUESDAY ___ / ___ / ___   RESTING HEART RATE _____ WEIGHT _____

DISTANCE _____   TIME _____   PACE/SPLITS _____   INTENSITY FACTOR _____

Notes _____

_____

_____

_____

ACHES AND PAINS _____

Rating	GREAT	VERY GOOD		GOOD	FAIR		POOR	VERY BAD
Nutrition	VEGGIE	FRUIT	GRAIN	MEAT/ FISH	NUT/SEED/ BEAN	WATER	SWEET	FRIED

10-second bursts once a week (preferably after you complete an easy run) will do the job.

WEDNESDAY ___ / ___ / ___   RESTING HEART RATE _____   WEIGHT _____

DISTANCE _____   TIME _____   PACE/SPLITS _____   INTENSITY FACTOR _____

Notes _____

_____

_____

_____

ACHES AND PAINS _____

Rating	GREAT	VERY GOOD		GOOD	FAIR		POOR	VERY BAD
Nutrition	VEGGIE	FRUIT	GRAIN	MEAT/ FISH	NUT/SEED/ BEAN	WATER	SWEET	FRIED

THURSDAY ___ / ___ / ___   RESTING HEART RATE _____   WEIGHT _____

DISTANCE _____   TIME _____   PACE/SPLITS _____   INTENSITY FACTOR _____

Notes _____

_____

_____

_____

ACHES AND PAINS _____

Rating	GREAT	VERY GOOD		GOOD	FAIR		POOR	VERY BAD
Nutrition	VEGGIE	FRUIT	GRAIN	MEAT/ FISH	NUT/SEED/ BEAN	WATER	SWEET	FRIED

FRIDAY ___ / ___ / ___

RESTING HEART RATE _____ WEIGHT _____

DISTANCE _____ TIME _____ PACE/SPLITS _____ INTENSITY FACTOR _____

Notes _____

_____

_____

_____

_____

ACHES AND PAINS _____

Rating	GREAT	VERY GOOD		GOOD	FAIR		POOR	VERY BAD
Nutrition	VEGGIE	FRUIT	GRAIN	MEAT/FISH	NUT/SEED/BEAN	WATER	SWEET	FRIED

SATURDAY ___ / ___ / ___

RESTING HEART RATE _____ WEIGHT _____

DISTANCE _____ TIME _____ PACE/SPLITS _____ INTENSITY FACTOR _____

Notes _____

_____

_____

_____

_____

ACHES AND PAINS _____

Rating	GREAT	VERY GOOD		GOOD	FAIR		POOR	VERY BAD
Nutrition	VEGGIE	FRUIT	GRAIN	MEAT/FISH	NUT/SEED/BEAN	WATER	SWEET	FRIED

SUNDAY ____ / ____ / ____

RESTING HEART RATE _____ WEIGHT _____

DISTANCE _____ TIME _____ PACE/SPLITS _____ INTENSITY FACTOR _____

Notes _____

_____

_____

_____

_____

_____

ACHES AND PAINS _____

Rating	GREAT	VERY GOOD		GOOD	FAIR		POOR	VERY BAD
Nutrition	VEGGIE	FRUIT	GRAIN	MEAT/ FISH	NUT/SEED/ BEAN	WATER	SWEET	FRIED

WEEKLY SUMMARY

AVERAGE INTENSITY FACTOR _____

	WEEKLY TOTAL	YEAR TO DATE
RUN DISTANCE		
RUN TIME		
OTHER TRAINING		
TOTAL TIME		

Notes _____

_____

_____

_____

_____

_____

MONDAY ___ / ___ / ___   RESTING HEART RATE _____ WEIGHT _____

DISTANCE _____   TIME _____   PACE/SPLITS _____   INTENSITY FACTOR _____

Notes _____

_____

_____

_____

ACHES AND PAINS _____

Rating	GREAT	VERY GOOD		GOOD	FAIR		POOR	VERY BAD
Nutrition	VEGGIE	FRUIT	GRAIN	MEAT/ FISH	NUT/SEED/ BEAN	WATER	SWEET	FRIED

TUESDAY ___ / ___ / ___   RESTING HEART RATE _____ WEIGHT _____

DISTANCE _____   TIME _____   PACE/SPLITS _____   INTENSITY FACTOR _____

Notes _____

_____

_____

_____

ACHES AND PAINS _____

Rating	GREAT	VERY GOOD		GOOD	FAIR		POOR	VERY BAD
Nutrition	VEGGIE	FRUIT	GRAIN	MEAT/ FISH	NUT/SEED/ BEAN	WATER	SWEET	FRIED

endurance of the breathing muscles by forcing the user to inhale and exhale against resistance.

WEDNESDAY ___ / ___ / ___   RESTING HEART RATE ___   WEIGHT ___

DISTANCE ___   TIME ___   PACE/SPLITS ___   INTENSITY FACTOR ___

Notes ___

___

___

___

ACHES AND PAINS ___

Rating	GREAT	VERY GOOD	GOOD	FAIR	POOR	VERY BAD

Nutrition	VEGGIE	FRUIT	GRAIN	MEAT/ FISH	NUT/SEED/ BEAN	WATER	SWEET	FRIED

THURSDAY ___ / ___ / ___   RESTING HEART RATE ___   WEIGHT ___

DISTANCE ___   TIME ___   PACE/SPLITS ___   INTENSITY FACTOR ___

Notes ___

___

___

___

ACHES AND PAINS ___

Rating	GREAT	VERY GOOD	GOOD	FAIR	POOR	VERY BAD

Nutrition	VEGGIE	FRUIT	GRAIN	MEAT/ FISH	NUT/SEED/ BEAN	WATER	SWEET	FRIED

FRIDAY ___ / ___ / ___

RESTING HEART RATE _____ WEIGHT _____

DISTANCE _____ TIME _____ PACE/SPLITS _____ INTENSITY FACTOR _____

Notes _____

_____

_____

_____

_____

ACHES AND PAINS _____

Rating	GREAT		VERY GOOD		GOOD		FAIR		POOR		VERY BAD
Nutrition	VEGGIE	FRUIT	GRAIN	MEAT/ FISH	NUT/SEED/ BEAN	WATER	SWEET	FRIED

SATURDAY ___ / ___ / ___

RESTING HEART RATE _____ WEIGHT _____

DISTANCE _____ TIME _____ PACE/SPLITS _____ INTENSITY FACTOR _____

Notes _____

_____

_____

_____

_____

ACHES AND PAINS _____

Rating	GREAT		VERY GOOD		GOOD		FAIR		POOR		VERY BAD
Nutrition	VEGGIE	FRUIT	GRAIN	MEAT/ FISH	NUT/SEED/ BEAN	WATER	SWEET	FRIED

SUNDAY ___ / ___ / ___

RESTING HEART RATE _____ WEIGHT _____

DISTANCE _____ TIME _____ PACE/SPLITS _____ INTENSITY FACTOR _____

Notes _____

_____

_____

_____

_____

ACHES AND PAINS _____

Rating	GREAT	VERY GOOD		GOOD	FAIR		POOR		VERY BAD
Nutrition	VEGGIE	FRUIT	GRAIN	MEAT/ FISH	NUT/SEED/ BEAN	WATER	SWEET	FRIED	

WEEKLY SUMMARY

AVERAGE INTENSITY FACTOR _____

	WEEKLY TOTAL	YEAR TO DATE
RUN DISTANCE		
RUN TIME		
OTHER TRAINING		
TOTAL TIME		

Notes _____

_____

_____

_____

_____

MONDAY	TUESDAY	WEDNESDAY	THURSDAY

FRIDAY   SATURDAY   SUNDAY

TOTAL DISTANCE

TOTAL DISTANCE

TOTAL DISTANCE

TOTAL DISTANCE

MONDAY ___ / ___ / ___   RESTING HEART RATE _____ WEIGHT _____

DISTANCE _____   TIME _____   PACE/SPLITS _____   INTENSITY FACTOR _____

Notes _____

_____

_____

_____

ACHES AND PAINS _____

Rating	GREAT	VERY GOOD		GOOD	FAIR		POOR	VERY BAD
Nutrition	VEGGIE	FRUIT	GRAIN	MEAT/ FISH	NUT/SEED/ BEAN	WATER	SWEET	FRIED

TUESDAY ___ / ___ / ___   RESTING HEART RATE _____ WEIGHT _____

DISTANCE _____   TIME _____   PACE/SPLITS _____   INTENSITY FACTOR _____

Notes _____

_____

_____

_____

ACHES AND PAINS _____

Rating	GREAT	VERY GOOD		GOOD	FAIR		POOR	VERY BAD
Nutrition	VEGGIE	FRUIT	GRAIN	MEAT/ FISH	NUT/SEED/ BEAN	WATER	SWEET	FRIED

you are left too tired to perform well in your next hard run. If you feel lousy, stop early to avoid sabotaging your next hard run.

WEDNESDAY ___/___/___   RESTING HEART RATE _____   WEIGHT _____

DISTANCE _____   TIME _____   PACE/SPLITS _____   INTENSITY FACTOR _____

Notes _____

_____

_____

_____

ACHES AND PAINS _____

Rating	GREAT	VERY GOOD		GOOD	FAIR		POOR	VERY BAD
Nutrition	VEGGIE	FRUIT	GRAIN	MEAT/ FISH	NUT/SEED/ BEAN	WATER	SWEET	FRIED

THURSDAY ___/___/___   RESTING HEART RATE _____   WEIGHT _____

DISTANCE _____   TIME _____   PACE/SPLITS _____   INTENSITY FACTOR _____

Notes _____

_____

_____

_____

ACHES AND PAINS _____

Rating	GREAT	VERY GOOD		GOOD	FAIR		POOR	VERY BAD
Nutrition	VEGGIE	FRUIT	GRAIN	MEAT/ FISH	NUT/SEED/ BEAN	WATER	SWEET	FRIED

FRIDAY ___ / ___ / ___

RESTING HEART RATE _____ WEIGHT _____

DISTANCE _____   TIME _____   PACE/SPLITS _____   INTENSITY FACTOR _____

Notes _____

_____

_____

_____

_____

ACHES AND PAINS _____

Rating	GREAT	VERY GOOD	GOOD	FAIR	POOR	VERY BAD

Nutrition	VEGGIE	FRUIT	GRAIN	MEAT/ FISH	NUT/SEED/ BEAN	WATER	SWEET	FRIED

SATURDAY ___ / ___ / ___

RESTING HEART RATE _____ WEIGHT _____

DISTANCE _____   TIME _____   PACE/SPLITS _____   INTENSITY FACTOR _____

Notes _____

_____

_____

_____

_____

ACHES AND PAINS _____

Rating	GREAT	VERY GOOD	GOOD	FAIR	POOR	VERY BAD

Nutrition	VEGGIE	FRUIT	GRAIN	MEAT/ FISH	NUT/SEED/ BEAN	WATER	SWEET	FRIED

SUNDAY ___ / ___ / ___

RESTING HEART RATE _____ WEIGHT _____

DISTANCE _____ TIME _____ PACE/SPLITS _____ INTENSITY FACTOR _____

Notes _____

_____

_____

_____

_____

ACHES AND PAINS _____

Rating	GREAT	VERY GOOD		GOOD	FAIR		POOR	VERY BAD
Nutrition	VEGGIE	FRUIT	GRAIN	MEAT/FISH	NUT/SEED/BEAN	WATER	SWEET	FRIED

WEEKLY SUMMARY

AVERAGE INTENSITY FACTOR _____

	WEEKLY TOTAL	YEAR TO DATE
RUN DISTANCE		
RUN TIME		
OTHER TRAINING		
TOTAL TIME		

Notes _____

_____

_____

_____

_____

MONDAY ___ / ___ / ___   RESTING HEART RATE _____ WEIGHT _____

DISTANCE _____   TIME _____   PACE/SPLITS _____   INTENSITY FACTOR _____

Notes _____

_____

_____

_____

ACHES AND PAINS _____

Rating	GREAT	VERY GOOD		GOOD	FAIR		POOR	VERY BAD
Nutrition	VEGGIE	FRUIT	GRAIN	MEAT/ FISH	NUT/SEED/ BEAN	WATER	SWEET	FRIED

TUESDAY ___ / ___ / ___   RESTING HEART RATE _____ WEIGHT _____

DISTANCE _____   TIME _____   PACE/SPLITS _____   INTENSITY FACTOR _____

Notes _____

_____

_____

_____

ACHES AND PAINS _____

Rating	GREAT	VERY GOOD		GOOD	FAIR		POOR	VERY BAD
Nutrition	VEGGIE	FRUIT	GRAIN	MEAT/ FISH	NUT/SEED/ BEAN	WATER	SWEET	FRIED

perform equally well on a diet containing anywhere from 50–75 percent carbohydrate, 20–40 percent fat, and 10–25 percent protein.

WEDNESDAY ___/___/___   RESTING HEART RATE _____ WEIGHT _____

DISTANCE _____   TIME _____   PACE/SPLITS _____   INTENSITY FACTOR _____

Notes _____

_____

_____

_____

ACHES AND PAINS _____

Rating	GREAT	VERY GOOD		GOOD	FAIR	POOR	VERY BAD
Nutrition	VEGGIE	FRUIT	GRAIN	MEAT/ FISH	NUT/SEED/ BEAN	WATER	SWEET	FRIED

THURSDAY ___/___/___   RESTING HEART RATE _____ WEIGHT _____

DISTANCE _____   TIME _____   PACE/SPLITS _____   INTENSITY FACTOR _____

Notes _____

_____

_____

_____

ACHES AND PAINS _____

Rating	GREAT	VERY GOOD		GOOD	FAIR	POOR	VERY BAD
Nutrition	VEGGIE	FRUIT	GRAIN	MEAT/ FISH	NUT/SEED/ BEAN	WATER	SWEET	FRIED

FRIDAY ___/___/___

RESTING HEART RATE _____ WEIGHT _____

DISTANCE _____   TIME _____   PACE/SPLITS _____   INTENSITY FACTOR _____

Notes _____

_____

_____

_____

_____

ACHES AND PAINS _____

Rating	GREAT	VERY GOOD	GOOD	FAIR	POOR	VERY BAD

Nutrition	VEGGIE	FRUIT	GRAIN	MEAT/ FISH	NUT/SEED/ BEAN	WATER	SWEET	FRIED

SATURDAY ___/___/___

RESTING HEART RATE _____ WEIGHT _____

DISTANCE _____   TIME _____   PACE/SPLITS _____   INTENSITY FACTOR _____

Notes _____

_____

_____

_____

_____

ACHES AND PAINS _____

Rating	GREAT	VERY GOOD	GOOD	FAIR	POOR	VERY BAD

Nutrition	VEGGIE	FRUIT	GRAIN	MEAT/ FISH	NUT/SEED/ BEAN	WATER	SWEET	FRIED

SUNDAY ___ / ___ / ___

RESTING HEART RATE _____ WEIGHT _____

DISTANCE _____ TIME _____ PACE/SPLITS _____ INTENSITY FACTOR _____

Notes _____

_____

_____

_____

_____

_____

ACHES AND PAINS _____

Rating	GREAT	VERY GOOD	GOOD	FAIR	POOR	VERY BAD

Nutrition	VEGGIE	FRUIT	GRAIN	MEAT/ FISH	NUT/SEED/ BEAN	WATER	SWEET	FRIED

WEEKLY SUMMARY

AVERAGE INTENSITY FACTOR _____

	WEEKLY TOTAL	YEAR TO DATE
RUN DISTANCE		
RUN TIME		
OTHER TRAINING		
TOTAL TIME		

Notes _____

_____

_____

_____

_____

MONDAY ___ / ___ / ___   RESTING HEART RATE _____ WEIGHT _____

DISTANCE _____   TIME _____   PACE/SPLITS _____   INTENSITY FACTOR _____

Notes _____

_____

_____

_____

ACHES AND PAINS _____

Rating	GREAT	VERY GOOD	GOOD	FAIR	POOR	VERY BAD
Nutrition	VEGGIE	FRUIT	GRAIN	MEAT/ FISH	NUT/SEED/ BEAN	WATER	SWEET	FRIED

TUESDAY ___ / ___ / ___   RESTING HEART RATE _____ WEIGHT _____

DISTANCE _____   TIME _____   PACE/SPLITS _____   INTENSITY FACTOR _____

Notes _____

_____

_____

_____

ACHES AND PAINS _____

Rating	GREAT	VERY GOOD	GOOD	FAIR	POOR	VERY BAD
Nutrition	VEGGIE	FRUIT	GRAIN	MEAT/ FISH	NUT/SEED/ BEAN	WATER	SWEET	FRIED

step. Lower that heel toward the floor and then contract your calf muscles to raise it again. Do this exercise with heavy dumbbells in your hands so that you can only do 8–10 repetitions.

WEDNESDAY ___ / ___ / ___   RESTING HEART RATE _____ WEIGHT _____

DISTANCE _____   TIME _____   PACE/SPLITS _____   INTENSITY FACTOR _____

Notes _____

_____

_____

_____

ACHES AND PAINS _____

Rating	GREAT	VERY GOOD	GOOD	FAIR	POOR	VERY BAD

Nutrition	VEGGIE	FRUIT	GRAIN	MEAT/FISH	NUT/SEED/BEAN	WATER	SWEET	FRIED

THURSDAY ___ / ___ / ___   RESTING HEART RATE _____ WEIGHT _____

DISTANCE _____   TIME _____   PACE/SPLITS _____   INTENSITY FACTOR _____

Notes _____

_____

_____

_____

ACHES AND PAINS _____

Rating	GREAT	VERY GOOD	GOOD	FAIR	POOR	VERY BAD

Nutrition	VEGGIE	FRUIT	GRAIN	MEAT/FISH	NUT/SEED/BEAN	WATER	SWEET	FRIED

FRIDAY ___ / ___ / ___

RESTING HEART RATE _____ WEIGHT _____

DISTANCE _____ TIME _____ PACE/SPLITS _____ INTENSITY FACTOR _____

Notes _____

_____

_____

_____

_____

ACHES AND PAINS _____

Rating	GREAT	VERY GOOD		GOOD	FAIR	POOR		VERY BAD
Nutrition	VEGGIE	FRUIT	GRAIN	MEAT/ FISH	NUT/SEED/ BEAN	WATER	SWEET	FRIED

SATURDAY ___ / ___ / ___

RESTING HEART RATE _____ WEIGHT _____

DISTANCE _____ TIME _____ PACE/SPLITS _____ INTENSITY FACTOR _____

Notes _____

_____

_____

_____

_____

ACHES AND PAINS _____

Rating	GREAT	VERY GOOD		GOOD	FAIR	POOR		VERY BAD
Nutrition	VEGGIE	FRUIT	GRAIN	MEAT/ FISH	NUT/SEED/ BEAN	WATER	SWEET	FRIED

SUNDAY ___ / ___ / ___

RESTING HEART RATE _____ WEIGHT _____

DISTANCE _____ TIME _____ PACE/SPLITS _____ INTENSITY FACTOR _____

Notes _____

_____

_____

_____

_____

_____

ACHES AND PAINS _____

Rating	GREAT	VERY GOOD	GOOD	FAIR	POOR	VERY BAD

Nutrition	VEGGIE	FRUIT	GRAIN	MEAT/ FISH	NUT/SEED/ BEAN	WATER	SWEET	FRIED

WEEKLY SUMMARY

AVERAGE INTENSITY FACTOR _____

	WEEKLY TOTAL	YEAR TO DATE
RUN DISTANCE		
RUN TIME		
OTHER TRAINING		
TOTAL TIME		

Notes _____

_____

_____

_____

_____

MONDAY ___ / ___ / ___   RESTING HEART RATE _____ WEIGHT _____

DISTANCE _____   TIME _____   PACE/SPLITS _____   INTENSITY FACTOR _____

Notes _____

_____

_____

_____

ACHES AND PAINS _____

Rating	GREAT	VERY GOOD	GOOD	FAIR	POOR	VERY BAD

Nutrition	VEGGIE	FRUIT	GRAIN	MEAT/ FISH	NUT/SEED/ BEAN	WATER	SWEET	FRIED

TUESDAY ___ / ___ / ___   RESTING HEART RATE _____ WEIGHT _____

DISTANCE _____   TIME _____   PACE/SPLITS _____   INTENSITY FACTOR _____

Notes _____

_____

_____

_____

ACHES AND PAINS _____

Rating	GREAT	VERY GOOD	GOOD	FAIR	POOR	VERY BAD

Nutrition	VEGGIE	FRUIT	GRAIN	MEAT/ FISH	NUT/SEED/ BEAN	WATER	SWEET	FRIED

(www.altitudetraining.com). By reducing the oxygen content of the air you breathe, these systems stimulate your body to create more oxygen-carrying blood cells, which could enhance your race performance by 2–4 percent.

WEDNESDAY ___ / ___ / ___   RESTING HEART RATE _____ WEIGHT _____

DISTANCE _____   TIME _____   PACE/SPLITS _____   INTENSITY FACTOR _____

Notes _____

_____

_____

_____

ACHES AND PAINS _____

Rating	GREAT	VERY GOOD	GOOD	FAIR	POOR	VERY BAD
Nutrition	VEGGIE	FRUIT	GRAIN	MEAT/FISH	NUT/SEED/BEAN	WATER	SWEET	FRIED

THURSDAY ___ / ___ / ___   RESTING HEART RATE _____ WEIGHT _____

DISTANCE _____   TIME _____   PACE/SPLITS _____   INTENSITY FACTOR _____

Notes _____

_____

_____

_____

ACHES AND PAINS _____

Rating	GREAT	VERY GOOD	GOOD	FAIR	POOR	VERY BAD
Nutrition	VEGGIE	FRUIT	GRAIN	MEAT/FISH	NUT/SEED/BEAN	WATER	SWEET	FRIED

FRIDAY ___ / ___ / ___

RESTING HEART RATE _____ WEIGHT _____

DISTANCE _____ TIME _____ PACE/SPLITS _____ INTENSITY FACTOR _____

Notes _____

_____

_____

_____

_____

ACHES AND PAINS _____

Rating	GREAT		VERY GOOD		GOOD		FAIR		POOR		VERY BAD
Nutrition	VEGGIE	FRUIT	GRAIN	MEAT/ FISH	NUT/SEED/ BEAN	WATER	SWEET	FRIED			

SATURDAY ___ / ___ / ___

RESTING HEART RATE _____ WEIGHT _____

DISTANCE _____ TIME _____ PACE/SPLITS _____ INTENSITY FACTOR _____

Notes _____

_____

_____

_____

_____

ACHES AND PAINS _____

Rating	GREAT		VERY GOOD		GOOD		FAIR		POOR		VERY BAD
Nutrition	VEGGIE	FRUIT	GRAIN	MEAT/ FISH	NUT/SEED/ BEAN	WATER	SWEET	FRIED			

SUNDAY ___ / ___ / ___

RESTING HEART RATE _____   WEIGHT _____

DISTANCE _____   TIME _____   PACE/SPLITS _____   INTENSITY FACTOR _____

Notes _____

_____

_____

_____

_____

_____

ACHES AND PAINS _____

Rating
| GREAT | VERY GOOD | GOOD | FAIR | POOR | VERY BAD |

Nutrition
| VEGGIE | FRUIT | GRAIN | MEAT/ FISH | NUT/SEED/ BEAN | WATER | SWEET | FRIED |

WEEKLY SUMMARY

AVERAGE INTENSITY FACTOR _____

	WEEKLY TOTAL	YEAR TO DATE
RUN DISTANCE		
RUN TIME		
OTHER TRAINING		
TOTAL TIME		

Notes _____

_____

_____

_____

_____

MONDAY	TUESDAY	WEDNESDAY	THURSDAY

FRIDAY	SATURDAY	SUNDAY	
			TOTAL DISTANCE
			TOTAL DISTANCE
			TOTAL DISTANCE
			TOTAL DISTANCE

MONDAY ___/___/___   RESTING HEART RATE _____ WEIGHT _____

DISTANCE _____   TIME _____   PACE/SPLITS _____   INTENSITY FACTOR _____

Notes_____

_____

_____

_____

ACHES AND PAINS _____

Rating	GREAT	VERY GOOD	GOOD	FAIR	POOR	VERY BAD

Nutrition	VEGGIE	FRUIT	GRAIN	MEAT/ FISH	NUT/SEED/ BEAN	WATER	SWEET	FRIED

TUESDAY ___/___/___   RESTING HEART RATE _____ WEIGHT _____

DISTANCE _____   TIME _____   PACE/SPLITS _____   INTENSITY FACTOR _____

Notes_____

_____

_____

_____

ACHES AND PAINS _____

Rating	GREAT	VERY GOOD	GOOD	FAIR	POOR	VERY BAD

Nutrition	VEGGIE	FRUIT	GRAIN	MEAT/ FISH	NUT/SEED/ BEAN	WATER	SWEET	FRIED

WEDNESDAY ___ / ___ / ___   RESTING HEART RATE _____   WEIGHT _____

DISTANCE _____   TIME _____   PACE/SPLITS _____   INTENSITY FACTOR _____

Notes _____

_____

_____

_____

ACHES AND PAINS _____

Rating	GREAT	VERY GOOD		GOOD	FAIR		POOR	VERY BAD
Nutrition	VEGGIE	FRUIT	GRAIN	MEAT/ FISH	NUT/SEED/ BEAN	WATER	SWEET	FRIED

THURSDAY ___ / ___ / ___   RESTING HEART RATE _____   WEIGHT _____

DISTANCE _____   TIME _____   PACE/SPLITS _____   INTENSITY FACTOR _____

Notes _____

_____

_____

_____

ACHES AND PAINS _____

Rating	GREAT	VERY GOOD		GOOD	FAIR		POOR	VERY BAD
Nutrition	VEGGIE	FRUIT	GRAIN	MEAT/ FISH	NUT/SEED/ BEAN	WATER	SWEET	FRIED

FRIDAY ___ / ___ / ___

RESTING HEART RATE _____ WEIGHT _____

DISTANCE _____ TIME _____ PACE/SPLITS _____ INTENSITY FACTOR _____

Notes _____

_____

_____

_____

_____

ACHES AND PAINS _____

Rating	GREAT	VERY GOOD	GOOD	FAIR	POOR	VERY BAD

Nutrition	VEGGIE	FRUIT	GRAIN	MEAT/ FISH	NUT/SEED/ BEAN	WATER	SWEET	FRIED

SATURDAY ___ / ___ / ___

RESTING HEART RATE _____ WEIGHT _____

DISTANCE _____ TIME _____ PACE/SPLITS _____ INTENSITY FACTOR _____

Notes _____

_____

_____

_____

_____

ACHES AND PAINS _____

Rating	GREAT	VERY GOOD	GOOD	FAIR	POOR	VERY BAD

Nutrition	VEGGIE	FRUIT	GRAIN	MEAT/ FISH	NUT/SEED/ BEAN	WATER	SWEET	FRIED

SUNDAY ___/___/___

RESTING HEART RATE _____ WEIGHT _____

DISTANCE _____ TIME _____ PACE/SPLITS _____ INTENSITY FACTOR _____

Notes _____

_____

_____

_____

_____

_____

ACHES AND PAINS _____

Rating	GREAT	VERY GOOD	GOOD	FAIR	POOR	VERY BAD

Nutrition	VEGGIE	FRUIT	GRAIN	MEAT/FISH	NUT/SEED/BEAN	WATER	SWEET	FRIED

WEEKLY SUMMARY

AVERAGE INTENSITY FACTOR _____

	WEEKLY TOTAL	YEAR TO DATE
RUN DISTANCE		
RUN TIME		
OTHER TRAINING		
TOTAL TIME		

Notes _____

_____

_____

_____

_____

MONDAY __ / __ / __   RESTING HEART RATE _____ WEIGHT _____

DISTANCE _____   TIME _____   PACE/SPLITS _____   INTENSITY FACTOR _____

Notes _____

_____

_____

_____

ACHES AND PAINS _____

Rating	GREAT		VERY GOOD		GOOD		FAIR		POOR		VERY BAD

Nutrition	VEGGIE	FRUIT	GRAIN	MEAT/ FISH	NUT/SEED/ BEAN	WATER	SWEET	FRIED

TUESDAY __ / __ / __   RESTING HEART RATE _____ WEIGHT _____

DISTANCE _____   TIME _____   PACE/SPLITS _____   INTENSITY FACTOR _____

Notes _____

_____

_____

_____

ACHES AND PAINS _____

Rating	GREAT		VERY GOOD		GOOD		FAIR		POOR		VERY BAD

Nutrition	VEGGIE	FRUIT	GRAIN	MEAT/ FISH	NUT/SEED/ BEAN	WATER	SWEET	FRIED

WEDNESDAY ___ / ___ / ___   RESTING HEART RATE _____ WEIGHT _____

DISTANCE _____   TIME _____   PACE/SPLITS _____   INTENSITY FACTOR _____

Notes _____

_____

_____

_____

ACHES AND PAINS _____

Rating	GREAT	VERY GOOD	GOOD	FAIR	POOR	VERY BAD

Nutrition	VEGGIE	FRUIT	GRAIN	MEAT/ FISH	NUT/SEED/ BEAN	WATER	SWEET	FRIED

THURSDAY ___ / ___ / ___   RESTING HEART RATE _____ WEIGHT _____

DISTANCE _____   TIME _____   PACE/SPLITS _____   INTENSITY FACTOR _____

Notes _____

_____

_____

_____

ACHES AND PAINS _____

Rating	GREAT	VERY GOOD	GOOD	FAIR	POOR	VERY BAD

Nutrition	VEGGIE	FRUIT	GRAIN	MEAT/ FISH	NUT/SEED/ BEAN	WATER	SWEET	FRIED

FRIDAY ___ / ___ / ___

RESTING HEART RATE _____ WEIGHT _____

DISTANCE _____ TIME _____ PACE/SPLITS _____ INTENSITY FACTOR _____

Notes _____

_____

_____

_____

_____

ACHES AND PAINS _____

| Rating | GREAT | VERY GOOD | GOOD | FAIR | POOR | VERY BAD |

| Nutrition | VEGGIE | FRUIT | GRAIN | MEAT/ FISH | NUT/SEED/ BEAN | WATER | SWEET | FRIED |

SATURDAY ___ / ___ / ___

RESTING HEART RATE _____ WEIGHT _____

DISTANCE _____ TIME _____ PACE/SPLITS _____ INTENSITY FACTOR _____

Notes _____

_____

_____

_____

_____

ACHES AND PAINS _____

| Rating | GREAT | VERY GOOD | GOOD | FAIR | POOR | VERY BAD |

| Nutrition | VEGGIE | FRUIT | GRAIN | MEAT/ FISH | NUT/SEED/ BEAN | WATER | SWEET | FRIED |

SUNDAY ___ / ___ / ___

RESTING HEART RATE _____ WEIGHT _____

DISTANCE _____ TIME _____ PACE/SPLITS _____ INTENSITY FACTOR _____

Notes _____

_____

_____

_____

_____

_____

ACHES AND PAINS _____

Rating	GREAT	VERY GOOD		GOOD	FAIR		POOR	VERY BAD
Nutrition	VEGGIE	FRUIT	GRAIN	MEAT/FISH	NUT/SEED/BEAN	WATER	SWEET	FRIED

WEEKLY SUMMARY

AVERAGE INTENSITY FACTOR _____

	WEEKLY TOTAL	YEAR TO DATE
RUN DISTANCE		
RUN TIME		
OTHER TRAINING		
TOTAL TIME		

Notes _____

_____

_____

_____

_____

109

MONDAY ___ / ___ / ___   RESTING HEART RATE _____ WEIGHT _____

DISTANCE _____   TIME _____   PACE/SPLITS _____   INTENSITY FACTOR _____

Notes _____

_____

_____

_____

ACHES AND PAINS _____

Rating   GREAT   VERY GOOD   GOOD   FAIR   POOR   VERY BAD

Nutrition   VEGGIE   FRUIT   GRAIN   MEAT/   NUT/SEED/   WATER   SWEET   FRIED
                                              FISH   BEAN

TUESDAY ___ / ___ / ___   RESTING HEART RATE _____ WEIGHT _____

DISTANCE _____   TIME _____   PACE/SPLITS _____   INTENSITY FACTOR _____

Notes _____

_____

_____

_____

ACHES AND PAINS _____

Rating   GREAT   VERY GOOD   GOOD   FAIR   POOR   VERY BAD

Nutrition   VEGGIE   FRUIT   GRAIN   MEAT/   NUT/SEED/   WATER   SWEET   FRIED
                                              FISH   BEAN

roller. Just lie with your injured side down on the foam roller and roll back and forth over the IT band from hip to knee.

WEDNESDAY ____ / ____ / ____   RESTING HEART RATE _____ WEIGHT _____

DISTANCE _____   TIME _____   PACE/SPLITS _____   INTENSITY FACTOR _____

Notes _____

_____

_____

_____

ACHES AND PAINS _____

Rating	GREAT	VERY GOOD		GOOD	FAIR		POOR	VERY BAD
Nutrition	VEGGIE	FRUIT	GRAIN	MEAT/ FISH	NUT/SEED/ BEAN	WATER	SWEET	FRIED

THURSDAY ____ / ____ / ____   RESTING HEART RATE _____ WEIGHT _____

DISTANCE _____   TIME _____   PACE/SPLITS _____   INTENSITY FACTOR _____

Notes _____

_____

_____

_____

ACHES AND PAINS _____

Rating	GREAT	VERY GOOD		GOOD	FAIR		POOR	VERY BAD
Nutrition	VEGGIE	FRUIT	GRAIN	MEAT/ FISH	NUT/SEED/ BEAN	WATER	SWEET	FRIED

FRIDAY ___ / ___ / ___

RESTING HEART RATE _____ WEIGHT _____

DISTANCE _____   TIME _____   PACE/SPLITS _____   INTENSITY FACTOR _____

Notes _____

_____

_____

_____

_____

ACHES AND PAINS _____

Rating	GREAT	VERY GOOD		GOOD	FAIR	POOR	VERY BAD

Nutrition	VEGGIE	FRUIT	GRAIN	MEAT/FISH	NUT/SEED/BEAN	WATER	SWEET	FRIED

SATURDAY ___ / ___ / ___

RESTING HEART RATE _____ WEIGHT _____

DISTANCE _____   TIME _____   PACE/SPLITS _____   INTENSITY FACTOR _____

Notes _____

_____

_____

_____

_____

ACHES AND PAINS _____

Rating	GREAT	VERY GOOD		GOOD	FAIR	POOR	VERY BAD

Nutrition	VEGGIE	FRUIT	GRAIN	MEAT/FISH	NUT/SEED/BEAN	WATER	SWEET	FRIED

SUNDAY ___ / ___ / ___

RESTING HEART RATE _____ WEIGHT _____

DISTANCE _____ TIME _____ PACE/SPLITS _____ INTENSITY FACTOR _____

Notes _____

_____

_____

_____

_____

ACHES AND PAINS _____

Rating | GREAT | VERY GOOD | GOOD | FAIR | POOR | VERY BAD

Nutrition	VEGGIE	FRUIT	GRAIN	MEAT/ FISH	NUT/SEED/ BEAN	WATER	SWEET	FRIED

WEEKLY SUMMARY

AVERAGE INTENSITY FACTOR _____

	WEEKLY TOTAL	YEAR TO DATE
RUN DISTANCE		
RUN TIME		
OTHER TRAINING		
TOTAL TIME		

Notes _____

_____

_____

_____

_____

MONDAY ___ / ___ / ___   RESTING HEART RATE _____ WEIGHT _____

DISTANCE _____   TIME _____   PACE/SPLITS _____   INTENSITY FACTOR _____

Notes _____

_____

_____

_____

ACHES AND PAINS _____

Rating

| GREAT | VERY GOOD | GOOD | FAIR | POOR | VERY BAD |

Nutrition

VEGGIE	FRUIT	GRAIN	MEAT/ FISH	NUT/SEED/ BEAN	WATER	SWEET	FRIED

TUESDAY ___ / ___ / ___   RESTING HEART RATE _____ WEIGHT _____

DISTANCE _____   TIME _____   PACE/SPLITS _____   INTENSITY FACTOR _____

Notes _____

_____

_____

_____

ACHES AND PAINS _____

Rating

| GREAT | VERY GOOD | GOOD | FAIR | POOR | VERY BAD |

Nutrition

VEGGIE	FRUIT	GRAIN	MEAT/ FISH	NUT/SEED/ BEAN	WATER	SWEET	FRIED

in a lunge position and pushing your sore hip forward until you feel a stretch on the front of the leg whose knee is touching the floor.

WEDNESDAY ___ / ___ / ___   RESTING HEART RATE _____ WEIGHT _____

DISTANCE _____   TIME _____   PACE/SPLITS _____   INTENSITY FACTOR _____

Notes _____

_____

_____

_____

ACHES AND PAINS _____

Rating	GREAT	VERY GOOD		GOOD	FAIR		POOR	VERY BAD
Nutrition	VEGGIE	FRUIT	GRAIN	MEAT/FISH	NUT/SEED/BEAN	WATER	SWEET	FRIED

THURSDAY ___ / ___ / ___   RESTING HEART RATE _____ WEIGHT _____

DISTANCE _____   TIME _____   PACE/SPLITS _____   INTENSITY FACTOR _____

Notes _____

_____

_____

_____

ACHES AND PAINS _____

Rating	GREAT	VERY GOOD		GOOD	FAIR		POOR	VERY BAD
Nutrition	VEGGIE	FRUIT	GRAIN	MEAT/FISH	NUT/SEED/BEAN	WATER	SWEET	FRIED

FRIDAY ___ / ___ / ___

RESTING HEART RATE _____ WEIGHT _____

DISTANCE _____ TIME _____ PACE/SPLITS _____ INTENSITY FACTOR _____

Notes _____

_____

_____

_____

_____

ACHES AND PAINS _____

Rating	GREAT		VERY GOOD		GOOD		FAIR		POOR		VERY BAD
Nutrition	VEGGIE	FRUIT	GRAIN	MEAT/ FISH	NUT/SEED/ BEAN	WATER	SWEET	FRIED

SATURDAY ___ / ___ / ___

RESTING HEART RATE _____ WEIGHT _____

DISTANCE _____ TIME _____ PACE/SPLITS _____ INTENSITY FACTOR _____

Notes _____

_____

_____

_____

_____

ACHES AND PAINS _____

Rating	GREAT		VERY GOOD		GOOD		FAIR		POOR		VERY BAD
Nutrition	VEGGIE	FRUIT	GRAIN	MEAT/ FISH	NUT/SEED/ BEAN	WATER	SWEET	FRIED

SUNDAY ___ / ___ / ___

RESTING HEART RATE _____ WEIGHT _____

DISTANCE _____ TIME _____ PACE/SPLITS _____ INTENSITY FACTOR _____

Notes _____

_____

_____

_____

_____

_____

ACHES AND PAINS _____

Rating	GREAT	VERY GOOD		GOOD	FAIR		POOR	VERY BAD
Nutrition	VEGGIE	FRUIT	GRAIN	MEAT/ FISH	NUT/SEED/ BEAN	WATER	SWEET	FRIED

WEEKLY SUMMARY

AVERAGE INTENSITY FACTOR _____

	WEEKLY TOTAL	YEAR TO DATE
RUN DISTANCE		
RUN TIME		
OTHER TRAINING		
TOTAL TIME		

Notes _____

_____

_____

_____

_____

MONDAY	TUESDAY	WEDNESDAY	THURSDAY

FRIDAY	SATURDAY	SUNDAY	
			TOTAL DISTANCE
			TOTAL DISTANCE
			TOTAL DISTANCE
			TOTAL DISTANCE

MONDAY ___ / ___ / ___   RESTING HEART RATE _____   WEIGHT _____

DISTANCE _____   TIME _____   PACE/SPLITS _____   INTENSITY FACTOR _____

Notes _____

_____

_____

_____

ACHES AND PAINS _____

Rating   GREAT   VERY GOOD   GOOD   FAIR   POOR   VERY BAD

Nutrition   VEGGIE   FRUIT   GRAIN   MEAT/ FISH   NUT/SEED/ BEAN   WATER   SWEET   FRIED

TUESDAY ___ / ___ / ___   RESTING HEART RATE _____   WEIGHT _____

DISTANCE _____   TIME _____   PACE/SPLITS _____   INTENSITY FACTOR _____

Notes _____

_____

_____

_____

ACHES AND PAINS _____

Rating   GREAT   VERY GOOD   GOOD   FAIR   POOR   VERY BAD

Nutrition   VEGGIE   FRUIT   GRAIN   MEAT/ FISH   NUT/SEED/ BEAN   WATER   SWEET   FRIED

training routine. Including giant walking lunges in your strength workouts can also help improve mobility.

WEDNESDAY ___ / ___ / ___   RESTING HEART RATE ___   WEIGHT ___

DISTANCE ___   TIME ___   PACE/SPLITS ___   INTENSITY FACTOR ___

Notes ___

___

___

___

ACHES AND PAINS ___

Rating

| GREAT | VERY GOOD | GOOD | FAIR | POOR | VERY BAD |

Nutrition

| VEGGIE | FRUIT | GRAIN | MEAT/FISH | NUT/SEED/BEAN | WATER | SWEET | FRIED |

THURSDAY ___ / ___ / ___   RESTING HEART RATE ___   WEIGHT ___

DISTANCE ___   TIME ___   PACE/SPLITS ___   INTENSITY FACTOR ___

Notes ___

___

___

___

ACHES AND PAINS ___

Rating

| GREAT | VERY GOOD | GOOD | FAIR | POOR | VERY BAD |

Nutrition

| VEGGIE | FRUIT | GRAIN | MEAT/FISH | NUT/SEED/BEAN | WATER | SWEET | FRIED |

FRIDAY ___ / ___ / ___

RESTING HEART RATE _____ WEIGHT _____

DISTANCE _____ TIME _____ PACE/SPLITS _____ INTENSITY FACTOR _____

Notes _____

_____

_____

_____

_____

ACHES AND PAINS _____

Rating	GREAT	VERY GOOD		GOOD		FAIR	POOR	VERY BAD
Nutrition	VEGGIE	FRUIT	GRAIN	MEAT/ FISH	NUT/SEED/ BEAN	WATER	SWEET	FRIED

SATURDAY ___ / ___ / ___

RESTING HEART RATE _____ WEIGHT _____

DISTANCE _____ TIME _____ PACE/SPLITS _____ INTENSITY FACTOR _____

Notes _____

_____

_____

_____

_____

ACHES AND PAINS _____

Rating	GREAT	VERY GOOD		GOOD		FAIR	POOR	VERY BAD
Nutrition	VEGGIE	FRUIT	GRAIN	MEAT/ FISH	NUT/SEED/ BEAN	WATER	SWEET	FRIED

SUNDAY ____ / ____ / ____

RESTING HEART RATE _____ WEIGHT _____

DISTANCE _____ TIME _____ PACE/SPLITS _____ INTENSITY FACTOR _____

Notes _____

_____

_____

_____

_____

ACHES AND PAINS _____

Rating

| GREAT | VERY GOOD | GOOD | FAIR | POOR | VERY BAD |

Nutrition

| VEGGIE | FRUIT | GRAIN | MEAT/FISH | NUT/SEED/BEAN | WATER | SWEET | FRIED |

WEEKLY SUMMARY

AVERAGE INTENSITY FACTOR _____

	WEEKLY TOTAL	YEAR TO DATE
RUN DISTANCE		
RUN TIME		
OTHER TRAINING		
TOTAL TIME		

Notes _____

_____

_____

_____

_____

MONDAY ___ / ___ / ___   RESTING HEART RATE _____ WEIGHT _____

DISTANCE _____   TIME _____   PACE/SPLITS _____   INTENSITY FACTOR _____

Notes _____

_____

_____

_____

ACHES AND PAINS _____

Rating	GREAT	VERY GOOD		GOOD	FAIR	POOR	VERY BAD
Nutrition	VEGGIE	FRUIT	GRAIN	MEAT/ FISH	NUT/SEED/ BEAN	WATER	SWEET	FRIED

TUESDAY ___ / ___ / ___   RESTING HEART RATE _____ WEIGHT _____

DISTANCE _____   TIME _____   PACE/SPLITS _____   INTENSITY FACTOR _____

Notes _____

_____

_____

_____

ACHES AND PAINS _____

Rating	GREAT	VERY GOOD		GOOD	FAIR	POOR	VERY BAD
Nutrition	VEGGIE	FRUIT	GRAIN	MEAT/ FISH	NUT/SEED/ BEAN	WATER	SWEET	FRIED

of your marathon without falling apart. The prefatigued time trial takes a lot out of you, so do it just one time 2–3 weeks before race day.

WEDNESDAY ___ / ___ / ___   RESTING HEART RATE ___   WEIGHT ___

DISTANCE ___   TIME ___   PACE/SPLITS ___   INTENSITY FACTOR ___

Notes ___

___

___

___

___

ACHES AND PAINS ___

Rating	GREAT	VERY GOOD	GOOD	FAIR	POOR	VERY BAD

Nutrition	VEGGIE	FRUIT	GRAIN	MEAT/FISH	NUT/SEED/BEAN	WATER	SWEET	FRIED

THURSDAY ___ / ___ / ___   RESTING HEART RATE ___   WEIGHT ___

DISTANCE ___   TIME ___   PACE/SPLITS ___   INTENSITY FACTOR ___

Notes ___

___

___

___

___

ACHES AND PAINS ___

Rating	GREAT	VERY GOOD	GOOD	FAIR	POOR	VERY BAD

Nutrition	VEGGIE	FRUIT	GRAIN	MEAT/FISH	NUT/SEED/BEAN	WATER	SWEET	FRIED

FRIDAY ___ / ___ / ___

RESTING HEART RATE _____ WEIGHT _____

DISTANCE _____ TIME _____ PACE/SPLITS _____ INTENSITY FACTOR _____

Notes _____

_____

_____

_____

_____

ACHES AND PAINS _____

Rating	GREAT	VERY GOOD	GOOD	FAIR	POOR	VERY BAD

Nutrition	VEGGIE	FRUIT	GRAIN	MEAT/FISH	NUT/SEED/BEAN	WATER	SWEET	FRIED

SATURDAY ___ / ___ / ___

RESTING HEART RATE _____ WEIGHT _____

DISTANCE _____ TIME _____ PACE/SPLITS _____ INTENSITY FACTOR _____

Notes _____

_____

_____

_____

_____

ACHES AND PAINS _____

Rating	GREAT	VERY GOOD	GOOD	FAIR	POOR	VERY BAD

Nutrition	VEGGIE	FRUIT	GRAIN	MEAT/FISH	NUT/SEED/BEAN	WATER	SWEET	FRIED

SUNDAY ___ / ___ / ___

RESTING HEART RATE _____ WEIGHT _____

DISTANCE _____ TIME _____ PACE/SPLITS _____ INTENSITY FACTOR _____

Notes _____

_____

_____

_____

_____

ACHES AND PAINS _____

Rating	GREAT	VERY GOOD		GOOD	FAIR		POOR	VERY BAD
Nutrition	VEGGIE	FRUIT	GRAIN	MEAT/ FISH	NUT/SEED/ BEAN	WATER	SWEET	FRIED

WEEKLY SUMMARY

AVERAGE INTENSITY FACTOR _____

	WEEKLY TOTAL	YEAR TO DATE
RUN DISTANCE		
RUN TIME		
OTHER TRAINING		
TOTAL TIME		

Notes _____

_____

_____

_____

_____

127

MONDAY ___ / ___ / ___   RESTING HEART RATE _____ WEIGHT _____

DISTANCE _____   TIME _____   PACE/SPLITS _____   INTENSITY FACTOR _____

Notes _____

_____

_____

_____

ACHES AND PAINS _____

Rating	GREAT	VERY GOOD	GOOD	FAIR	POOR	VERY BAD

Nutrition	VEGGIE	FRUIT	GRAIN	MEAT/ FISH	NUT/SEED/ BEAN	WATER	SWEET	FRIED

TUESDAY ___ / ___ / ___   RESTING HEART RATE _____ WEIGHT _____

DISTANCE _____   TIME _____   PACE/SPLITS _____   INTENSITY FACTOR _____

Notes _____

_____

_____

_____

ACHES AND PAINS _____

Rating	GREAT	VERY GOOD	GOOD	FAIR	POOR	VERY BAD

Nutrition	VEGGIE	FRUIT	GRAIN	MEAT/ FISH	NUT/SEED/ BEAN	WATER	SWEET	FRIED

whatsoever between fruit juice consumption and being overweight, and in fact those who consume 100 percent fruit juice regularly tend to have higher insulin sensitivity (which is a good thing) than those who drink it less often.

WEDNESDAY ___ / ___ / ___   RESTING HEART RATE ___   WEIGHT ___

DISTANCE ___   TIME ___   PACE/SPLITS ___   INTENSITY FACTOR ___

Notes ___

___

___

___

ACHES AND PAINS ___

Rating	GREAT	VERY GOOD		GOOD	FAIR	POOR	VERY BAD
Nutrition	VEGGIE	FRUIT	GRAIN	MEAT/ FISH	NUT/SEED/ BEAN	WATER	SWEET	FRIED

THURSDAY ___ / ___ / ___   RESTING HEART RATE ___   WEIGHT ___

DISTANCE ___   TIME ___   PACE/SPLITS ___   INTENSITY FACTOR ___

Notes ___

___

___

___

ACHES AND PAINS ___

Rating	GREAT	VERY GOOD		GOOD	FAIR	POOR	VERY BAD
Nutrition	VEGGIE	FRUIT	GRAIN	MEAT/ FISH	NUT/SEED/ BEAN	WATER	SWEET	FRIED

FRIDAY ___/___/___

RESTING HEART RATE _____ WEIGHT _____

DISTANCE _____ TIME _____ PACE/SPLITS _____ INTENSITY FACTOR _____

Notes _____

_____

_____

_____

_____

ACHES AND PAINS _____

Rating	GREAT	VERY GOOD		GOOD	FAIR		POOR	VERY BAD
Nutrition	VEGGIE	FRUIT	GRAIN	MEAT/FISH	NUT/SEED/BEAN	WATER	SWEET	FRIED

SATURDAY ___/___/___

RESTING HEART RATE _____ WEIGHT _____

DISTANCE _____ TIME _____ PACE/SPLITS _____ INTENSITY FACTOR _____

Notes _____

_____

_____

_____

_____

ACHES AND PAINS _____

Rating	GREAT	VERY GOOD		GOOD	FAIR		POOR	VERY BAD
Nutrition	VEGGIE	FRUIT	GRAIN	MEAT/FISH	NUT/SEED/BEAN	WATER	SWEET	FRIED

SUNDAY ___ / ___ / ___

RESTING HEART RATE _____ WEIGHT _____

DISTANCE _____ TIME _____ PACE/SPLITS _____ INTENSITY FACTOR _____

Notes _____

_____

_____

_____

_____

ACHES AND PAINS _____

Rating	GREAT	VERY GOOD		GOOD	FAIR	POOR		VERY BAD
Nutrition	VEGGIE	FRUIT	GRAIN	MEAT/ FISH	NUT/SEED/ BEAN	WATER	SWEET	FRIED

WEEKLY SUMMARY

AVERAGE INTENSITY FACTOR _____

	WEEKLY TOTAL	YEAR TO DATE
RUN DISTANCE		
RUN TIME		
OTHER TRAINING		
TOTAL TIME		

Notes _____

_____

_____

_____

_____

MONDAY ___/___/___

RESTING HEART RATE _____ WEIGHT _____

DISTANCE _____ TIME _____ PACE/SPLITS _____ INTENSITY FACTOR _____

Notes _____

_____

_____

_____

ACHES AND PAINS _____

Rating	GREAT	VERY GOOD	GOOD	FAIR	POOR	VERY BAD

Nutrition	VEGGIE	FRUIT	GRAIN	MEAT/ FISH	NUT/SEED/ BEAN	WATER	SWEET	FRIED

TUESDAY ___/___/___

RESTING HEART RATE _____ WEIGHT _____

DISTANCE _____ TIME _____ PACE/SPLITS _____ INTENSITY FACTOR _____

Notes _____

_____

_____

_____

ACHES AND PAINS _____

Rating	GREAT	VERY GOOD	GOOD	FAIR	POOR	VERY BAD

Nutrition	VEGGIE	FRUIT	GRAIN	MEAT/ FISH	NUT/SEED/ BEAN	WATER	SWEET	FRIED

workout to test your fitness, such as 3 x 1 mile at 10K race pace. If your performance is in line with where you were before you got injured, then resume your normal training. Otherwise, scale it back appropriately.

WEDNESDAY ___ / ___ / ___   RESTING HEART RATE _____   WEIGHT _____

DISTANCE _____   TIME _____   PACE/SPLITS _____   INTENSITY FACTOR _____

Notes _____

_____

_____

_____

ACHES AND PAINS _____

Rating	GREAT	VERY GOOD		GOOD	FAIR		POOR	VERY BAD
Nutrition	VEGGIE	FRUIT	GRAIN	MEAT/FISH	NUT/SEED/BEAN	WATER	SWEET	FRIED

THURSDAY ___ / ___ / ___   RESTING HEART RATE _____   WEIGHT _____

DISTANCE _____   TIME _____   PACE/SPLITS _____   INTENSITY FACTOR _____

Notes _____

_____

_____

_____

ACHES AND PAINS _____

Rating	GREAT	VERY GOOD		GOOD	FAIR		POOR	VERY BAD
Nutrition	VEGGIE	FRUIT	GRAIN	MEAT/FISH	NUT/SEED/BEAN	WATER	SWEET	FRIED

FRIDAY ____ / ____ / ____

RESTING HEART RATE _____ WEIGHT _____

DISTANCE _____ TIME _____ PACE/SPLITS _____ INTENSITY FACTOR _____

Notes _____

_____

_____

_____

_____

ACHES AND PAINS _____

Rating	GREAT		VERY GOOD		GOOD		FAIR		POOR		VERY BAD

Nutrition	VEGGIE	FRUIT	GRAIN	MEAT/ FISH	NUT/SEED/ BEAN	WATER	SWEET	FRIED

SATURDAY ____ / ____ / ____

RESTING HEART RATE _____ WEIGHT _____

DISTANCE _____ TIME _____ PACE/SPLITS _____ INTENSITY FACTOR _____

Notes _____

_____

_____

_____

_____

ACHES AND PAINS _____

Rating	GREAT		VERY GOOD		GOOD		FAIR		POOR		VERY BAD

Nutrition	VEGGIE	FRUIT	GRAIN	MEAT/ FISH	NUT/SEED/ BEAN	WATER	SWEET	FRIED

SUNDAY ___ / ___ / ___

RESTING HEART RATE _____ WEIGHT _____

DISTANCE _____ TIME _____ PACE/SPLITS _____ INTENSITY FACTOR _____

Notes _____

_____

_____

_____

_____

_____

ACHES AND PAINS _____

Rating	GREAT	VERY GOOD	GOOD	FAIR	POOR	VERY BAD

Nutrition	VEGGIE	FRUIT	GRAIN	MEAT/ FISH	NUT/SEED/ BEAN	WATER	SWEET	FRIED

WEEKLY SUMMARY

AVERAGE INTENSITY FACTOR _____

	WEEKLY TOTAL	YEAR TO DATE
RUN DISTANCE		
RUN TIME		
OTHER TRAINING		
TOTAL TIME		

Notes _____

_____

_____

_____

_____

MONDAY	TUESDAY	WEDNESDAY	THURSDAY

FRIDAY   SATURDAY   SUNDAY

TOTAL DISTANCE

TOTAL DISTANCE

TOTAL DISTANCE

TOTAL DISTANCE

MONDAY ___/___/___   RESTING HEART RATE _____ WEIGHT _____

DISTANCE _____   TIME _____   PACE/SPLITS _____   INTENSITY FACTOR _____

Notes _____

_____

_____

_____

ACHES AND PAINS _____

Rating	GREAT	VERY GOOD	GOOD	FAIR	POOR	VERY BAD

Nutrition	VEGGIE	FRUIT	GRAIN	MEAT/ FISH	NUT/SEED/ BEAN	WATER	SWEET	FRIED

TUESDAY ___/___/___   RESTING HEART RATE _____ WEIGHT _____

DISTANCE _____   TIME _____   PACE/SPLITS _____   INTENSITY FACTOR _____

Notes _____

_____

_____

_____

ACHES AND PAINS _____

Rating	GREAT	VERY GOOD	GOOD	FAIR	POOR	VERY BAD

Nutrition	VEGGIE	FRUIT	GRAIN	MEAT/ FISH	NUT/SEED/ BEAN	WATER	SWEET	FRIED

of possibilities such as enabling you to perform speed workouts with intervals of precise distances without the need to find a track to run on.

WEDNESDAY ___/___/___   RESTING HEART RATE _____ WEIGHT _____

DISTANCE _____   TIME _____   PACE/SPLITS _____   INTENSITY FACTOR _____

Notes _____

_____

_____

_____

ACHES AND PAINS _____

Rating	GREAT	VERY GOOD		GOOD	FAIR	POOR		VERY BAD
Nutrition	VEGGIE	FRUIT	GRAIN	MEAT/FISH	NUT/SEED/BEAN	WATER	SWEET	FRIED

THURSDAY ___/___/___   RESTING HEART RATE _____ WEIGHT _____

DISTANCE _____   TIME _____   PACE/SPLITS _____   INTENSITY FACTOR _____

Notes _____

_____

_____

_____

ACHES AND PAINS _____

Rating	GREAT	VERY GOOD		GOOD	FAIR	POOR		VERY BAD
Nutrition	VEGGIE	FRUIT	GRAIN	MEAT/FISH	NUT/SEED/BEAN	WATER	SWEET	FRIED

139

FRIDAY ___ / ___ / ___

RESTING HEART RATE _____ WEIGHT _____

DISTANCE _____ TIME _____ PACE/SPLITS _____ INTENSITY FACTOR _____

Notes _____

_____

_____

_____

_____

ACHES AND PAINS _____

Rating

| GREAT | VERY GOOD | GOOD | FAIR | POOR | VERY BAD |

Nutrition

VEGGIE	FRUIT	GRAIN	MEAT/FISH	NUT/SEED/BEAN	WATER	SWEET	FRIED

SATURDAY ___ / ___ / ___

RESTING HEART RATE _____ WEIGHT _____

DISTANCE _____ TIME _____ PACE/SPLITS _____ INTENSITY FACTOR _____

Notes _____

_____

_____

_____

_____

ACHES AND PAINS _____

Rating

| GREAT | VERY GOOD | GOOD | FAIR | POOR | VERY BAD |

Nutrition

VEGGIE	FRUIT	GRAIN	MEAT/FISH	NUT/SEED/BEAN	WATER	SWEET	FRIED

SUNDAY ___ / ___ / ___

RESTING HEART RATE _____ WEIGHT _____

DISTANCE _____ TIME _____ PACE/SPLITS _____ INTENSITY FACTOR _____

Notes _____

_____

_____

_____

_____

_____

ACHES AND PAINS _____

Rating	GREAT	VERY GOOD	GOOD	FAIR	POOR	VERY BAD

Nutrition	VEGGIE	FRUIT	GRAIN	MEAT/ FISH	NUT/SEED/ BEAN	WATER	SWEET	FRIED

WEEKLY SUMMARY

AVERAGE INTENSITY FACTOR _____

	WEEKLY TOTAL	YEAR TO DATE
RUN DISTANCE		
RUN TIME		
OTHER TRAINING		
TOTAL TIME		

Notes _____

_____

_____

_____

_____

MONDAY ___/___/___   RESTING HEART RATE _____ WEIGHT _____

DISTANCE _____   TIME _____   PACE/SPLITS _____   INTENSITY FACTOR _____

Notes _____

_____

_____

_____

ACHES AND PAINS _____

Rating	GREAT		VERY GOOD		GOOD		FAIR		POOR		VERY BAD

Nutrition	VEGGIE	FRUIT	GRAIN	MEAT/ FISH	NUT/SEED/ BEAN	WATER	SWEET	FRIED

TUESDAY ___/___/___   RESTING HEART RATE _____ WEIGHT _____

DISTANCE _____   TIME _____   PACE/SPLITS _____   INTENSITY FACTOR _____

Notes _____

_____

_____

_____

ACHES AND PAINS _____

Rating	GREAT		VERY GOOD		GOOD		FAIR		POOR		VERY BAD

Nutrition	VEGGIE	FRUIT	GRAIN	MEAT/ FISH	NUT/SEED/ BEAN	WATER	SWEET	FRIED

your muscles' radical-fighting capacity, but a diet based on antioxidant-rich fruits and vegetables will also help significantly.

WEDNESDAY ___ / ___ / ___   RESTING HEART RATE _____   WEIGHT _____

DISTANCE _____   TIME _____   PACE/SPLITS _____   INTENSITY FACTOR _____

Notes _____

_____

_____

_____

ACHES AND PAINS _____

Rating	GREAT	VERY GOOD		GOOD	FAIR	POOR	VERY BAD

Nutrition	VEGGIE	FRUIT	GRAIN	MEAT/FISH	NUT/SEED/BEAN	WATER	SWEET	FRIED

THURSDAY ___ / ___ / ___   RESTING HEART RATE _____   WEIGHT _____

DISTANCE _____   TIME _____   PACE/SPLITS _____   INTENSITY FACTOR _____

Notes _____

_____

_____

_____

ACHES AND PAINS _____

Rating	GREAT	VERY GOOD		GOOD	FAIR	POOR	VERY BAD

Nutrition	VEGGIE	FRUIT	GRAIN	MEAT/FISH	NUT/SEED/BEAN	WATER	SWEET	FRIED

FRIDAY ___/___/___

RESTING HEART RATE _____ WEIGHT _____

DISTANCE _____   TIME _____   PACE/SPLITS _____   INTENSITY FACTOR _____

Notes _____
_____
_____
_____
_____

ACHES AND PAINS _____

Rating   GREAT   VERY GOOD   GOOD   FAIR   POOR   VERY BAD

Nutrition	VEGGIE	FRUIT	GRAIN	MEAT/ FISH	NUT/SEED/ BEAN	WATER	SWEET	FRIED

SATURDAY ___/___/___

RESTING HEART RATE _____ WEIGHT _____

DISTANCE _____   TIME _____   PACE/SPLITS _____   INTENSITY FACTOR _____

Notes _____
_____
_____
_____
_____

ACHES AND PAINS _____

Rating   GREAT   VERY GOOD   GOOD   FAIR   POOR   VERY BAD

Nutrition	VEGGIE	FRUIT	GRAIN	MEAT/ FISH	NUT/SEED/ BEAN	WATER	SWEET	FRIED

SUNDAY ___ / ___ / ___

RESTING HEART RATE _____ WEIGHT _____

DISTANCE _____ TIME _____ PACE/SPLITS _____ INTENSITY FACTOR _____

Notes _____

_____

_____

_____

_____

_____

ACHES AND PAINS _____

Rating	GREAT	VERY GOOD	GOOD	FAIR	POOR	VERY BAD
Nutrition	VEGGIE	FRUIT	GRAIN	MEAT/FISH	NUT/SEED/BEAN	WATER	SWEET	FRIED

WEEKLY SUMMARY

AVERAGE INTENSITY FACTOR _____

	WEEKLY TOTAL	YEAR TO DATE
RUN DISTANCE		
RUN TIME		
OTHER TRAINING		
TOTAL TIME		

Notes _____

_____

_____

_____

_____

MONDAY _____ / _____ / _____   RESTING HEART RATE _____ WEIGHT _____

DISTANCE _____   TIME _____   PACE/SPLITS _____   INTENSITY FACTOR _____

Notes _____

_____

_____

_____

ACHES AND PAINS _____

Rating
| GREAT | VERY GOOD | GOOD | FAIR | POOR | VERY BAD |

Nutrition
| VEGGIE | FRUIT | GRAIN | MEAT/ FISH | NUT/SEED/ BEAN | WATER | SWEET | FRIED |

TUESDAY _____ / _____ / _____   RESTING HEART RATE _____ WEIGHT _____

DISTANCE _____   TIME _____   PACE/SPLITS _____   INTENSITY FACTOR _____

Notes _____

_____

_____

_____

ACHES AND PAINS _____

Rating
| GREAT | VERY GOOD | GOOD | FAIR | POOR | VERY BAD |

Nutrition
| VEGGIE | FRUIT | GRAIN | MEAT/ FISH | NUT/SEED/ BEAN | WATER | SWEET | FRIED |

free to specialize in shorter races—especially if you enjoy them more. Prove your seriousness not by going long but by going fast!

WEDNESDAY ___/___/___   RESTING HEART RATE _____ WEIGHT _____

DISTANCE _____   TIME _____   PACE/SPLITS _____   INTENSITY FACTOR _____

Notes _____
_____
_____
_____

ACHES AND PAINS _____

Rating	GREAT	VERY GOOD	GOOD	FAIR	POOR	VERY BAD

Nutrition	VEGGIE	FRUIT	GRAIN	MEAT/FISH	NUT/SEED/BEAN	WATER	SWEET	FRIED

THURSDAY ___/___/___   RESTING HEART RATE _____ WEIGHT _____

DISTANCE _____   TIME _____   PACE/SPLITS _____   INTENSITY FACTOR _____

Notes _____
_____
_____
_____

ACHES AND PAINS _____

Rating	GREAT	VERY GOOD	GOOD	FAIR	POOR	VERY BAD

Nutrition	VEGGIE	FRUIT	GRAIN	MEAT/FISH	NUT/SEED/BEAN	WATER	SWEET	FRIED

FRIDAY ___ / ___ / ___

RESTING HEART RATE _____ WEIGHT _____

DISTANCE _____ TIME _____ PACE/SPLITS _____ INTENSITY FACTOR _____

Notes _____

_____

_____

_____

_____

ACHES AND PAINS _____

Rating	GREAT	VERY GOOD	GOOD	FAIR	POOR	VERY BAD

Nutrition	VEGGIE	FRUIT	GRAIN	MEAT/ FISH	NUT/SEED/ BEAN	WATER	SWEET	FRIED

SATURDAY ___ / ___ / ___

RESTING HEART RATE _____ WEIGHT _____

DISTANCE _____ TIME _____ PACE/SPLITS _____ INTENSITY FACTOR _____

Notes _____

_____

_____

_____

_____

ACHES AND PAINS _____

Rating	GREAT	VERY GOOD	GOOD	FAIR	POOR	VERY BAD

Nutrition	VEGGIE	FRUIT	GRAIN	MEAT/ FISH	NUT/SEED/ BEAN	WATER	SWEET	FRIED

SUNDAY ___ / ___ / ___

RESTING HEART RATE _____ WEIGHT _____

DISTANCE _____ TIME _____ PACE/SPLITS _____ INTENSITY FACTOR _____

Notes _____

_____

_____

_____

_____

_____

ACHES AND PAINS _____

Rating	GREAT	VERY GOOD	GOOD	FAIR	POOR	VERY BAD

Nutrition	VEGGIE	FRUIT	GRAIN	MEAT/FISH	NUT/SEED/BEAN	WATER	SWEET	FRIED

WEEKLY SUMMARY

AVERAGE INTENSITY FACTOR _____

	WEEKLY TOTAL	YEAR TO DATE
RUN DISTANCE		
RUN TIME		
OTHER TRAINING		
TOTAL TIME		

Notes _____

_____

_____

_____

_____

MONDAY ___ / ___ / ___   RESTING HEART RATE _____ WEIGHT _____

DISTANCE _____   TIME _____   PACE/SPLITS _____   INTENSITY FACTOR _____

Notes _____

_____

_____

_____

ACHES AND PAINS _____

Rating	GREAT	VERY GOOD		GOOD	FAIR		POOR	VERY BAD
Nutrition	VEGGIE	FRUIT	GRAIN	MEAT/ FISH	NUT/SEED/ BEAN	WATER	SWEET	FRIED

TUESDAY ___ / ___ / ___   RESTING HEART RATE _____ WEIGHT _____

DISTANCE _____   TIME _____   PACE/SPLITS _____   INTENSITY FACTOR _____

Notes _____

_____

_____

_____

ACHES AND PAINS _____

Rating	GREAT	VERY GOOD		GOOD	FAIR		POOR	VERY BAD
Nutrition	VEGGIE	FRUIT	GRAIN	MEAT/ FISH	NUT/SEED/ BEAN	WATER	SWEET	FRIED

Many runners get a significant boost from running just a couple of miles in the morning and saving their longer runs for the afternoon.

WEDNESDAY ___ / ___ / ___   RESTING HEART RATE ___   WEIGHT ___

DISTANCE ___   TIME ___   PACE/SPLITS ___   INTENSITY FACTOR ___

Notes ___

___

___

___

ACHES AND PAINS ___

Rating	GREAT	VERY GOOD	GOOD	FAIR	POOR	VERY BAD

Nutrition	VEGGIE	FRUIT	GRAIN	MEAT/ FISH	NUT/SEED/ BEAN	WATER	SWEET	FRIED

THURSDAY ___ / ___ / ___   RESTING HEART RATE ___   WEIGHT ___

DISTANCE ___   TIME ___   PACE/SPLITS ___   INTENSITY FACTOR ___

Notes ___

___

___

___

ACHES AND PAINS ___

Rating	GREAT	VERY GOOD	GOOD	FAIR	POOR	VERY BAD

Nutrition	VEGGIE	FRUIT	GRAIN	MEAT/ FISH	NUT/SEED/ BEAN	WATER	SWEET	FRIED

FRIDAY ___ / ___ / ___

RESTING HEART RATE _____ WEIGHT _____

DISTANCE _____ TIME _____ PACE/SPLITS _____ INTENSITY FACTOR _____

Notes _____

_____

_____

_____

_____

ACHES AND PAINS _____

Rating	GREAT	VERY GOOD	GOOD	FAIR	POOR	VERY BAD

Nutrition	VEGGIE	FRUIT	GRAIN	MEAT/FISH	NUT/SEED/BEAN	WATER	SWEET	FRIED

SATURDAY ___ / ___ / ___

RESTING HEART RATE _____ WEIGHT _____

DISTANCE _____ TIME _____ PACE/SPLITS _____ INTENSITY FACTOR _____

Notes _____

_____

_____

_____

_____

ACHES AND PAINS _____

Rating	GREAT	VERY GOOD	GOOD	FAIR	POOR	VERY BAD

Nutrition	VEGGIE	FRUIT	GRAIN	MEAT/FISH	NUT/SEED/BEAN	WATER	SWEET	FRIED

SUNDAY ____ / ____ / ____

RESTING HEART RATE _____ WEIGHT _____

DISTANCE _____ TIME _____ PACE/SPLITS _____ INTENSITY FACTOR _____

Notes _____

_____

_____

_____

_____

_____

ACHES AND PAINS _____

Rating	GREAT	VERY GOOD	GOOD	FAIR	POOR	VERY BAD

Nutrition	VEGGIE	FRUIT	GRAIN	MEAT/FISH	NUT/SEED/BEAN	WATER	SWEET	FRIED

WEEKLY SUMMARY

AVERAGE INTENSITY FACTOR _____

	WEEKLY TOTAL	YEAR TO DATE
RUN DISTANCE		
RUN TIME		
OTHER TRAINING		
TOTAL TIME		

Notes _____

_____

_____

_____

_____

MONDAY	TUESDAY	WEDNESDAY	THURSDAY

FRIDAY	SATURDAY	SUNDAY	
			TOTAL DISTANCE
			TOTAL DISTANCE
			TOTAL DISTANCE
			TOTAL DISTANCE

MONDAY ___ / ___ / ___   RESTING HEART RATE _____ WEIGHT _____

DISTANCE _____   TIME _____   PACE/SPLITS _____   INTENSITY FACTOR _____

Notes _____

_____

_____

_____

ACHES AND PAINS _____

Rating   GREAT   VERY GOOD   GOOD   FAIR   POOR   VERY BAD

Nutrition	VEGGIE	FRUIT	GRAIN	MEAT/ FISH	NUT/SEED/ BEAN	WATER	SWEET	FRIED

TUESDAY ___ / ___ / ___   RESTING HEART RATE _____ WEIGHT _____

DISTANCE _____   TIME _____   PACE/SPLITS _____   INTENSITY FACTOR _____

Notes _____

_____

_____

_____

ACHES AND PAINS _____

Rating   GREAT   VERY GOOD   GOOD   FAIR   POOR   VERY BAD

Nutrition	VEGGIE	FRUIT	GRAIN	MEAT/ FISH	NUT/SEED/ BEAN	WATER	SWEET	FRIED

will not get your heart rate as high as you do when running, but it's much easier on the legs.

WEDNESDAY ___/___/___ RESTING HEART RATE _____ WEIGHT _____

DISTANCE _____ TIME _____ PACE/SPLITS _____ INTENSITY FACTOR _____

Notes _____

_____

_____

_____

ACHES AND PAINS _____

Rating	GREAT	VERY GOOD	GOOD	FAIR	POOR	VERY BAD

Nutrition	VEGGIE	FRUIT	GRAIN	MEAT/FISH	NUT/SEED/BEAN	WATER	SWEET	FRIED

THURSDAY ___/___/___ RESTING HEART RATE _____ WEIGHT _____

DISTANCE _____ TIME _____ PACE/SPLITS _____ INTENSITY FACTOR _____

Notes _____

_____

_____

_____

ACHES AND PAINS _____

Rating	GREAT	VERY GOOD	GOOD	FAIR	POOR	VERY BAD

Nutrition	VEGGIE	FRUIT	GRAIN	MEAT/FISH	NUT/SEED/BEAN	WATER	SWEET	FRIED

FRIDAY ___ / ___ / ___

RESTING HEART RATE _____ WEIGHT _____

DISTANCE _____ TIME _____ PACE/SPLITS _____ INTENSITY FACTOR _____

Notes _____

_____

_____

_____

_____

ACHES AND PAINS _____

Rating	GREAT		VERY GOOD		GOOD		FAIR		POOR		VERY BAD
Nutrition	VEGGIE	FRUIT	GRAIN	MEAT/FISH	NUT/SEED/BEAN	WATER	SWEET	FRIED

SATURDAY ___ / ___ / ___

RESTING HEART RATE _____ WEIGHT _____

DISTANCE _____ TIME _____ PACE/SPLITS _____ INTENSITY FACTOR _____

Notes _____

_____

_____

_____

_____

ACHES AND PAINS _____

Rating	GREAT		VERY GOOD		GOOD		FAIR		POOR		VERY BAD
Nutrition	VEGGIE	FRUIT	GRAIN	MEAT/FISH	NUT/SEED/BEAN	WATER	SWEET	FRIED

SUNDAY ___ / ___ / ___

RESTING HEART RATE _____ WEIGHT _____

DISTANCE _____ TIME _____ PACE/SPLITS _____ INTENSITY FACTOR _____

Notes _____

_____

_____

_____

_____

_____

ACHES AND PAINS _____

Rating	GREAT	VERY GOOD	GOOD	FAIR	POOR	VERY BAD

Nutrition	VEGGIE	FRUIT	GRAIN	MEAT/ FISH	NUT/SEED/ BEAN	WATER	SWEET	FRIED

WEEKLY SUMMARY

AVERAGE INTENSITY FACTOR _____

	WEEKLY TOTAL	YEAR TO DATE
RUN DISTANCE		
RUN TIME		
OTHER TRAINING		
TOTAL TIME		

Notes _____

_____

_____

_____

_____

MONDAY ___/___/___   RESTING HEART RATE _____ WEIGHT _____

DISTANCE _____   TIME _____   PACE/SPLITS _____   INTENSITY FACTOR _____

Notes _____

_____

_____

_____

ACHES AND PAINS _____

Rating	GREAT	VERY GOOD		GOOD	FAIR		POOR	VERY BAD
Nutrition	VEGGIE	FRUIT	GRAIN	MEAT/ FISH	NUT/SEED/ BEAN	WATER	SWEET	FRIED

TUESDAY ___/___/___   RESTING HEART RATE _____ WEIGHT _____

DISTANCE _____   TIME _____   PACE/SPLITS _____   INTENSITY FACTOR _____

Notes _____

_____

_____

_____

ACHES AND PAINS _____

Rating	GREAT	VERY GOOD		GOOD	FAIR		POOR	VERY BAD
Nutrition	VEGGIE	FRUIT	GRAIN	MEAT/ FISH	NUT/SEED/ BEAN	WATER	SWEET	FRIED

4–6 days of light training is plenty, but very-high-mileage runners should begin to reduce their training progressively 10–14 days before competing.

WEDNESDAY ___ / ___ / ___   RESTING HEART RATE ___   WEIGHT ___

DISTANCE ___   TIME ___   PACE/SPLITS ___   INTENSITY FACTOR ___

Notes _____

_____

_____

_____

ACHES AND PAINS _____

Rating	GREAT	VERY GOOD	GOOD	FAIR	POOR	VERY BAD

Nutrition	VEGGIE	FRUIT	GRAIN	MEAT/ FISH	NUT/SEED/ BEAN	WATER	SWEET	FRIED

THURSDAY ___ / ___ / ___   RESTING HEART RATE ___   WEIGHT ___

DISTANCE ___   TIME ___   PACE/SPLITS ___   INTENSITY FACTOR ___

Notes _____

_____

_____

_____

ACHES AND PAINS _____

Rating	GREAT	VERY GOOD	GOOD	FAIR	POOR	VERY BAD

Nutrition	VEGGIE	FRUIT	GRAIN	MEAT/ FISH	NUT/SEED/ BEAN	WATER	SWEET	FRIED

FRIDAY ___/___/___

RESTING HEART RATE _____ WEIGHT _____

DISTANCE _____ TIME _____ PACE/SPLITS _____ INTENSITY FACTOR _____

Notes _____

_____

_____

_____

_____

ACHES AND PAINS _____

Rating	GREAT		VERY GOOD		GOOD		FAIR		POOR		VERY BAD
Nutrition	VEGGIE	FRUIT	GRAIN	MEAT/FISH	NUT/SEED/BEAN	WATER	SWEET	FRIED

SATURDAY ___/___/___

RESTING HEART RATE _____ WEIGHT _____

DISTANCE _____ TIME _____ PACE/SPLITS _____ INTENSITY FACTOR _____

Notes _____

_____

_____

_____

_____

ACHES AND PAINS _____

Rating	GREAT		VERY GOOD		GOOD		FAIR		POOR		VERY BAD
Nutrition	VEGGIE	FRUIT	GRAIN	MEAT/FISH	NUT/SEED/BEAN	WATER	SWEET	FRIED

SUNDAY ___ / ___ / ___

RESTING HEART RATE _____ WEIGHT _____

DISTANCE _____ TIME _____ PACE/SPLITS _____ INTENSITY FACTOR

Notes _____

_____

_____

_____

_____

_____

ACHES AND PAINS _____

Rating	GREAT	VERY GOOD		GOOD		FAIR	POOR		VERY BAD
Nutrition	VEGGIE	FRUIT	GRAIN	MEAT/ FISH	NUT/SEED/ BEAN	WATER		SWEET	FRIED

WEEKLY SUMMARY

AVERAGE INTENSITY FACTOR _____

	WEEKLY TOTAL	YEAR TO DATE
RUN DISTANCE		
RUN TIME		
OTHER TRAINING		
TOTAL TIME		

Notes _____

_____

_____

_____

_____

MONDAY ___ / ___ / ___   RESTING HEART RATE ___   WEIGHT ___

DISTANCE ___   TIME ___   PACE/SPLITS ___   INTENSITY FACTOR ___

Notes _____

_____

_____

_____

ACHES AND PAINS _____

Rating   GREAT   VERY GOOD   GOOD   FAIR   POOR   VERY BAD

Nutrition	VEGGIE	FRUIT	GRAIN	MEAT/FISH	NUT/SEED/BEAN	WATER	SWEET	FRIED

TUESDAY ___ / ___ / ___   RESTING HEART RATE ___   WEIGHT ___

DISTANCE ___   TIME ___   PACE/SPLITS ___   INTENSITY FACTOR ___

Notes _____

_____

_____

_____

ACHES AND PAINS _____

Rating   GREAT   VERY GOOD   GOOD   FAIR   POOR   VERY BAD

Nutrition	VEGGIE	FRUIT	GRAIN	MEAT/FISH	NUT/SEED/BEAN	WATER	SWEET	FRIED

exposure to running in a fatigued state, which is a potent stimulator of fitness adaptations. So cool down whenever you have time, but don't worry if you have to skip it every once in a while.

WEDNESDAY ___ / ___ / ___   RESTING HEART RATE _____   WEIGHT _____

DISTANCE _____   TIME _____   PACE/SPLITS _____   INTENSITY FACTOR _____

Notes _____

_____

_____

_____

ACHES AND PAINS _____

Rating	GREAT	VERY GOOD		GOOD	FAIR		POOR	VERY BAD

Nutrition	VEGGIE	FRUIT	GRAIN	MEAT/ FISH	NUT/SEED/ BEAN	WATER	SWEET	FRIED

THURSDAY __ / ___ / ___   RESTING HEART RATE _____   WEIGHT _____

DISTANCE _____   TIME _____   PACE/SPLITS _____   INTENSITY FACTOR _____

Notes _____

_____

_____

_____

ACHES AND PAINS _____

Rating	GREAT	VERY GOOD		GOOD	FAIR		POOR	VERY BAD

Nutrition	VEGGIE	FRUIT	GRAIN	MEAT/ FISH	NUT/SEED/ BEAN	WATER	SWEET	FRIED

FRIDAY ___ / ___ / ___

RESTING HEART RATE _____ WEIGHT _____

DISTANCE _____ TIME _____ PACE/SPLITS _____ INTENSITY FACTOR _____

Notes _____

_____

_____

_____

_____

_____

ACHES AND PAINS _____

Rating	GREAT	VERY GOOD		GOOD	FAIR		POOR	VERY BAD
Nutrition	VEGGIE	FRUIT	GRAIN	MEAT/ FISH	NUT/SEED/ BEAN	WATER	SWEET	FRIED

SATURDAY ___ / ___ / ___

RESTING HEART RATE _____ WEIGHT _____

DISTANCE _____ TIME _____ PACE/SPLITS _____ INTENSITY FACTOR _____

Notes _____

_____

_____

_____

_____

_____

ACHES AND PAINS _____

Rating	GREAT	VERY GOOD		GOOD	FAIR		POOR	VERY BAD
Nutrition	VEGGIE	FRUIT	GRAIN	MEAT/ FISH	NUT/SEED/ BEAN	WATER	SWEET	FRIED

SUNDAY ___ / ___ / ___

RESTING HEART RATE _____ WEIGHT _____

DISTANCE _____ TIME _____ PACE/SPLITS _____ INTENSITY FACTOR _____

Notes _____

_____

_____

_____

_____

ACHES AND PAINS _____

Rating	GREAT	VERY GOOD	GOOD	FAIR	POOR	VERY BAD

Nutrition	VEGGIE	FRUIT	GRAIN	MEAT/ FISH	NUT/SEED/ BEAN	WATER	SWEET	FRIED

WEEKLY SUMMARY

AVERAGE INTENSITY FACTOR _____

	WEEKLY TOTAL	YEAR TO DATE
RUN DISTANCE		
RUN TIME		
OTHER TRAINING		
TOTAL TIME		

Notes _____

_____

_____

_____

_____

167

MONDAY ___ / ___ / ___   RESTING HEART RATE _____ WEIGHT _____

DISTANCE _____   TIME _____   PACE/SPLITS _____   INTENSITY FACTOR _____

Notes _____

_____

_____

_____

ACHES AND PAINS _____

Rating   GREAT   VERY GOOD   GOOD   FAIR   POOR   VERY BAD

Nutrition   VEGGIE   FRUIT   GRAIN   MEAT/FISH   NUT/SEED/BEAN   WATER   SWEET   FRIED

TUESDAY ___ / ___ / ___   RESTING HEART RATE _____ WEIGHT _____

DISTANCE _____   TIME _____   PACE/SPLITS _____   INTENSITY FACTOR _____

Notes _____

_____

_____

_____

ACHES AND PAINS _____

Rating   GREAT   VERY GOOD   GOOD   FAIR   POOR   VERY BAD

Nutrition   VEGGIE   FRUIT   GRAIN   MEAT/FISH   NUT/SEED/BEAN   WATER   SWEET   FRIED

distance. There are several good calculators out there, but my favorite is that of coach Greg McMillan, which you can find at www.mcmillanrunning.com.

WEDNESDAY ___/___/___   RESTING HEART RATE _____ WEIGHT _____

DISTANCE _____   TIME _____   PACE/SPLITS _____   INTENSITY FACTOR _____

Notes _____

_____

_____

_____

ACHES AND PAINS _____

Rating	GREAT	VERY GOOD		GOOD	FAIR		POOR	VERY BAD
Nutrition	VEGGIE	FRUIT	GRAIN	MEAT/FISH	NUT/SEED/BEAN	WATER	SWEET	FRIED

THURSDAY ___/___/___   RESTING HEART RATE _____ WEIGHT _____

DISTANCE _____   TIME _____   PACE/SPLITS _____   INTENSITY FACTOR _____

Notes _____

_____

_____

_____

ACHES AND PAINS _____

Rating	GREAT	VERY GOOD		GOOD	FAIR		POOR	VERY BAD
Nutrition	VEGGIE	FRUIT	GRAIN	MEAT/FISH	NUT/SEED/BEAN	WATER	SWEET	FRIED

FRIDAY ___ / ___ / ___

RESTING HEART RATE _____ WEIGHT _____

DISTANCE _____ TIME _____ PACE/SPLITS _____ INTENSITY FACTOR _____

Notes _____

_____

_____

_____

_____

ACHES AND PAINS _____

Rating	GREAT	VERY GOOD	GOOD	FAIR	POOR	VERY BAD
Nutrition	VEGGIE	FRUIT	GRAIN	MEAT/FISH	NUT/SEED/BEAN	WATER	SWEET	FRIED

SATURDAY ___ / ___ / ___

RESTING HEART RATE _____ WEIGHT _____

DISTANCE _____ TIME _____ PACE/SPLITS _____ INTENSITY FACTOR _____

Notes _____

_____

_____

_____

_____

ACHES AND PAINS _____

Rating	GREAT	VERY GOOD	GOOD	FAIR	POOR	VERY BAD
Nutrition	VEGGIE	FRUIT	GRAIN	MEAT/FISH	NUT/SEED/BEAN	WATER	SWEET	FRIED

SUNDAY ___/___/___

RESTING HEART RATE _____ WEIGHT _____

DISTANCE _____ TIME _____ PACE/SPLITS _____ INTENSITY FACTOR _____

Notes _____

_____

_____

_____

_____

ACHES AND PAINS _____

Rating	GREAT	VERY GOOD	GOOD	FAIR	POOR	VERY BAD

Nutrition	VEGGIE	FRUIT	GRAIN	MEAT/FISH	NUT/SEED/BEAN	WATER	SWEET	FRIED

WEEKLY SUMMARY

AVERAGE INTENSITY FACTOR _____

	WEEKLY TOTAL	YEAR TO DATE
RUN DISTANCE		
RUN TIME		
OTHER TRAINING		
TOTAL TIME		

Notes _____

_____

_____

_____

_____

MONDAY	TUESDAY	WEDNESDAY	THURSDAY

FRIDAY   SATURDAY   SUNDAY

TOTAL DISTANCE

TOTAL DISTANCE

TOTAL DISTANCE

TOTAL DISTANCE

MONDAY ___ / ___ / ___   RESTING HEART RATE _____ WEIGHT _____

DISTANCE _____   TIME _____   PACE/SPLITS _____   INTENSITY FACTOR _____

Notes _____

_____

_____

_____

ACHES AND PAINS _____

Rating	GREAT	VERY GOOD		GOOD	FAIR		POOR	VERY BAD
Nutrition	VEGGIE	FRUIT	GRAIN	MEAT/ FISH	NUT/SEED/ BEAN	WATER	SWEET	FRIED

TUESDAY ___ / ___ / ___   RESTING HEART RATE _____ WEIGHT _____

DISTANCE _____   TIME _____   PACE/SPLITS _____   INTENSITY FACTOR _____

Notes _____

_____

_____

_____

ACHES AND PAINS _____

Rating	GREAT	VERY GOOD		GOOD	FAIR		POOR	VERY BAD
Nutrition	VEGGIE	FRUIT	GRAIN	MEAT/ FISH	NUT/SEED/ BEAN	WATER	SWEET	FRIED

Stepping on the floor in the morning stretches the tissue once more and undoes the healing. To overcome this problem, sleep in a therapeutic night splint that keeps your fascia stretched as you sleep.

WEDNESDAY ___/___/___   RESTING HEART RATE _____ WEIGHT _____

DISTANCE _____   TIME _____   PACE/SPLITS _____   INTENSITY FACTOR _____

Notes _____

_____

_____

_____

ACHES AND PAINS _____

Rating	GREAT	VERY GOOD	GOOD	FAIR	POOR	VERY BAD

Nutrition	VEGGIE	FRUIT	GRAIN	MEAT/FISH	NUT/SEED/BEAN	WATER	SWEET	FRIED

THURSDAY ___/___/___   RESTING HEART RATE _____ WEIGHT _____

DISTANCE _____   TIME _____   PACE/SPLITS _____   INTENSITY FACTOR _____

Notes _____

_____

_____

_____

ACHES AND PAINS _____

Rating	GREAT	VERY GOOD	GOOD	FAIR	POOR	VERY BAD

Nutrition	VEGGIE	FRUIT	GRAIN	MEAT/FISH	NUT/SEED/BEAN	WATER	SWEET	FRIED

FRIDAY ___ / ___ / ___

RESTING HEART RATE _____ WEIGHT _____

DISTANCE _____ TIME _____ PACE/SPLITS _____ INTENSITY FACTOR _____

Notes _____

_____

_____

_____

_____

ACHES AND PAINS _____

Rating	GREAT	VERY GOOD	GOOD	FAIR	POOR	VERY BAD

Nutrition	VEGGIE	FRUIT	GRAIN	MEAT/FISH	NUT/SEED/BEAN	WATER	SWEET	FRIED

SATURDAY ___ / ___ / ___

RESTING HEART RATE _____ WEIGHT _____

DISTANCE _____ TIME _____ PACE/SPLITS _____ INTENSITY FACTOR _____

Notes _____

_____

_____

_____

_____

ACHES AND PAINS _____

Rating	GREAT	VERY GOOD	GOOD	FAIR	POOR	VERY BAD

Nutrition	VEGGIE	FRUIT	GRAIN	MEAT/FISH	NUT/SEED/BEAN	WATER	SWEET	FRIED

SUNDAY ___/___/___

RESTING HEART RATE _____ WEIGHT _____

DISTANCE _____ TIME _____ PACE/SPLITS _____ INTENSITY FACTOR _____

Notes _____

_____

_____

_____

_____

ACHES AND PAINS _____

Rating	GREAT		VERY GOOD		GOOD	FAIR		POOR		VERY BAD
Nutrition	VEGGIE	FRUIT	GRAIN	MEAT/FISH	NUT/SEED/BEAN	WATER	SWEET	FRIED		

WEEKLY SUMMARY

AVERAGE INTENSITY FACTOR _____

	WEEKLY TOTAL	YEAR TO DATE
RUN DISTANCE		
RUN TIME		
OTHER TRAINING		
TOTAL TIME		

Notes _____

_____

_____

_____

_____

177

MONDAY ___ / ___ / ___   RESTING HEART RATE ___   WEIGHT ___

DISTANCE ___   TIME ___   PACE/SPLITS ___   INTENSITY FACTOR ___

Notes ___

___

___

___

ACHES AND PAINS ___

Rating	GREAT	VERY GOOD	GOOD	FAIR	POOR	VERY BAD

Nutrition	VEGGIE	FRUIT	GRAIN	MEAT/FISH	NUT/SEED/BEAN	WATER	SWEET	FRIED

TUESDAY ___ / ___ / ___   RESTING HEART RATE ___   WEIGHT ___

DISTANCE ___   TIME ___   PACE/SPLITS ___   INTENSITY FACTOR ___

Notes ___

___

___

___

ACHES AND PAINS ___

Rating	GREAT	VERY GOOD	GOOD	FAIR	POOR	VERY BAD

Nutrition	VEGGIE	FRUIT	GRAIN	MEAT/FISH	NUT/SEED/BEAN	WATER	SWEET	FRIED

178

done 6–8 total sprints. If you can still stand, cool down with a couple more minutes of jogging. As short as it is, this brutally intense workout is proven to give aerobic and anaerobic capacity a huge boost.

WEDNESDAY ___ / ___ / ___   RESTING HEART RATE _____   WEIGHT _____

DISTANCE _____   TIME _____   PACE/SPLITS _____   INTENSITY FACTOR _____

Notes _____

_____

_____

_____

ACHES AND PAINS _____

Rating	GREAT	VERY GOOD		GOOD	FAIR	POOR		VERY BAD
Nutrition	VEGGIE	FRUIT	GRAIN	MEAT/ FISH	NUT/SEED/ BEAN	WATER	SWEET	FRIED

THURSDAY ___ / ___ / ___   RESTING HEART RATE _____   WEIGHT _____

DISTANCE _____   TIME _____   PACE/SPLITS _____   INTENSITY FACTOR _____

Notes _____

_____

_____

_____

ACHES AND PAINS _____

Rating	GREAT	VERY GOOD		GOOD	FAIR	POOR		VERY BAD
Nutrition	VEGGIE	FRUIT	GRAIN	MEAT/ FISH	NUT/SEED/ BEAN	WATER	SWEET	FRIED

FRIDAY ____/____/____

RESTING HEART RATE _____ WEIGHT _____

DISTANCE _____ TIME _____ PACE/SPLITS _____ INTENSITY FACTOR _____

Notes _____

_____

_____

_____

_____

ACHES AND PAINS _____

Rating

GREAT	VERY GOOD	GOOD	FAIR	POOR	VERY BAD

Nutrition

VEGGIE	FRUIT	GRAIN	MEAT/FISH	NUT/SEED/BEAN	WATER	SWEET	FRIED

SATURDAY ____/____/____

RESTING HEART RATE _____ WEIGHT _____

DISTANCE _____ TIME _____ PACE/SPLITS _____ INTENSITY FACTOR _____

Notes _____

_____

_____

_____

_____

ACHES AND PAINS _____

Rating

GREAT	VERY GOOD	GOOD	FAIR	POOR	VERY BAD

Nutrition

VEGGIE	FRUIT	GRAIN	MEAT/FISH	NUT/SEED/BEAN	WATER	SWEET	FRIED

SUNDAY ___ / ___ / ___

RESTING HEART RATE _____ WEIGHT _____

DISTANCE _____ TIME _____ PACE/SPLITS _____ INTENSITY FACTOR _____

Notes _____

_____

_____

_____

_____

_____

ACHES AND PAINS _____

Rating	GREAT	VERY GOOD		GOOD	FAIR		POOR	VERY BAD
Nutrition	VEGGIE	FRUIT	GRAIN	MEAT/ FISH	NUT/SEED/ BEAN	WATER	SWEET	FRIED

WEEKLY SUMMARY

AVERAGE INTENSITY FACTOR _____

	WEEKLY TOTAL	YEAR TO DATE
RUN DISTANCE		
RUN TIME		
OTHER TRAINING		
TOTAL TIME		

Notes _____

_____

_____

_____

_____

MONDAY ___ / ___ / ___   RESTING HEART RATE _____ WEIGHT _____

DISTANCE _____   TIME _____   PACE/SPLITS _____   INTENSITY FACTOR _____

Notes _____

_____

_____

_____

ACHES AND PAINS _____

Rating	GREAT		VERY GOOD		GOOD		FAIR		POOR		VERY BAD
Nutrition	VEGGIE	FRUIT	GRAIN	MEAT/ FISH	NUT/SEED/ BEAN	WATER	SWEET	FRIED

TUESDAY ___ / ___ / ___   RESTING HEART RATE _____ WEIGHT _____

DISTANCE _____   TIME _____   PACE/SPLITS _____   INTENSITY FACTOR _____

Notes _____

_____

_____

_____

ACHES AND PAINS _____

Rating	GREAT		VERY GOOD		GOOD		FAIR		POOR		VERY BAD
Nutrition	VEGGIE	FRUIT	GRAIN	MEAT/ FISH	NUT/SEED/ BEAN	WATER	SWEET	FRIED

excellent day-to-day hydration despite seldom drinking during or immediately after runs, but instead drinking according to their thirst. You can also expect to stay hydrated by trusting your thirst.

WEDNESDAY ___/___/___   RESTING HEART RATE _____ WEIGHT _____

DISTANCE _____   TIME _____   PACE/SPLITS _____   INTENSITY FACTOR _____

Notes _____
_____
_____
_____

ACHES AND PAINS _____

Rating	GREAT	VERY GOOD		GOOD	FAIR	POOR	VERY BAD

Nutrition	VEGGIE	FRUIT	GRAIN	MEAT/ FISH	NUT/SEED/ BEAN	WATER	SWEET	FRIED

THURSDAY ___/___/___   RESTING HEART RATE _____ WEIGHT _____

DISTANCE _____   TIME _____   PACE/SPLITS _____   INTENSITY FACTOR _____

Notes _____
_____
_____
_____

ACHES AND PAINS _____

Rating	GREAT	VERY GOOD		GOOD	FAIR	POOR	VERY BAD

Nutrition	VEGGIE	FRUIT	GRAIN	MEAT/ FISH	NUT/SEED/ BEAN	WATER	SWEET	FRIED

FRIDAY ___ / ___ / ___

RESTING HEART RATE _____ WEIGHT _____

DISTANCE _____ TIME _____ PACE/SPLITS _____ INTENSITY FACTOR _____

Notes _____

_____

_____

_____

_____

ACHES AND PAINS _____

Rating

GREAT	VERY GOOD	GOOD	FAIR	POOR	VERY BAD

Nutrition

VEGGIE	FRUIT	GRAIN	MEAT/ FISH	NUT/SEED/ BEAN	WATER	SWEET	FRIED

SATURDAY ___ / ___ / ___

RESTING HEART RATE _____ WEIGHT _____

DISTANCE _____ TIME _____ PACE/SPLITS _____ INTENSITY FACTOR _____

Notes _____

_____

_____

_____

_____

ACHES AND PAINS _____

Rating

GREAT	VERY GOOD	GOOD	FAIR	POOR	VERY BAD

Nutrition

VEGGIE	FRUIT	GRAIN	MEAT/ FISH	NUT/SEED/ BEAN	WATER	SWEET	FRIED

SUNDAY ___ / ___ / ___   RESTING HEART RATE _____ WEIGHT _____

DISTANCE _____   TIME _____   PACE/SPLITS _____   INTENSITY FACTOR _____

Notes _____

_____

_____

_____

_____

ACHES AND PAINS _____

Rating	GREAT	VERY GOOD	GOOD	FAIR	POOR	VERY BAD

Nutrition	VEGGIE	FRUIT	GRAIN	MEAT/FISH	NUT/SEED/BEAN	WATER	SWEET	FRIED

WEEKLY SUMMARY   AVERAGE INTENSITY FACTOR _____

	WEEKLY TOTAL	YEAR TO DATE
RUN DISTANCE		
RUN TIME		
OTHER TRAINING		
TOTAL TIME		

Notes _____

_____

_____

_____

_____

MONDAY ___ / ___ / ___   RESTING HEART RATE _____ WEIGHT _____

DISTANCE _____   TIME _____   PACE/SPLITS _____   INTENSITY FACTOR _____

Notes _____

_____

_____

_____

ACHES AND PAINS _____

Rating	GREAT	VERY GOOD	GOOD	FAIR	POOR	VERY BAD

Nutrition	VEGGIE	FRUIT	GRAIN	MEAT/ FISH	NUT/SEED/ BEAN	WATER	SWEET	FRIED

TUESDAY ___ / ___ / ___   RESTING HEART RATE _____ WEIGHT _____

DISTANCE _____   TIME _____   PACE/SPLITS _____   INTENSITY FACTOR _____

Notes _____

_____

_____

_____

ACHES AND PAINS _____

Rating	GREAT	VERY GOOD	GOOD	FAIR	POOR	VERY BAD

Nutrition	VEGGIE	FRUIT	GRAIN	MEAT/ FISH	NUT/SEED/ BEAN	WATER	SWEET	FRIED

performance. The faster you go, the better the effect. So be sure to include some fast downhill running in your weekly training routine.

WEDNESDAY ____ / ____ / ____   RESTING HEART RATE _____   WEIGHT _____

DISTANCE _____   TIME _____   PACE/SPLITS _____   INTENSITY FACTOR _____

Notes _____

_____

_____

_____

ACHES AND PAINS _____

Rating   GREAT   VERY GOOD   GOOD   FAIR   POOR   VERY BAD

Nutrition   VEGGIE   FRUIT   GRAIN   MEAT/   NUT/SEED/   WATER   SWEET   FRIED
                                        FISH   BEAN

THURSDAY ____ / ____ / ____   RESTING HEART RATE _____   WEIGHT _____

DISTANCE _____   TIME _____   PACE/SPLITS _____   INTENSITY FACTOR _____

Notes _____

_____

_____

_____

ACHES AND PAINS _____

Rating   GREAT   VERY GOOD   GOOD   FAIR   POOR   VERY BAD

Nutrition   VEGGIE   FRUIT   GRAIN   MEAT/   NUT/SEED/   WATER   SWEET   FRIED
                                        FISH   BEAN

FRIDAY ___ / ___ / ___

RESTING HEART RATE _____   WEIGHT _____

DISTANCE _____   TIME _____   PACE/SPLITS _____   INTENSITY FACTOR _____

Notes _____

_____

_____

_____

_____

ACHES AND PAINS _____

Rating   GREAT   VERY GOOD   GOOD   FAIR   POOR   VERY BAD

Nutrition   VEGGIE   FRUIT   GRAIN   MEAT/   NUT/SEED/   WATER   SWEET   FRIED
                                               FISH   BEAN

SATURDAY ___ / ___ / ___

RESTING HEART RATE _____   WEIGHT _____

DISTANCE _____   TIME _____   PACE/SPLITS _____   INTENSITY FACTOR _____

Notes _____

_____

_____

_____

_____

ACHES AND PAINS _____

Rating   GREAT   VERY GOOD   GOOD   FAIR   POOR   VERY BAD

Nutrition   VEGGIE   FRUIT   GRAIN   MEAT/   NUT/SEED/   WATER   SWEET   FRIED
                                               FISH   BEAN

SUNDAY ___ / ___ / ___

RESTING HEART RATE _____ WEIGHT _____

DISTANCE _____ TIME _____ PACE/SPLITS _____ INTENSITY FACTOR _____

Notes _____

_____

_____

_____

_____

_____

ACHES AND PAINS _____

Rating	GREAT	VERY GOOD	GOOD	FAIR	POOR	VERY BAD

Nutrition	VEGGIE	FRUIT	GRAIN	MEAT/FISH	NUT/SEED/BEAN	WATER	SWEET	FRIED

WEEKLY SUMMARY

AVERAGE INTENSITY FACTOR _____

	WEEKLY TOTAL	YEAR TO DATE
RUN DISTANCE		
RUN TIME		
OTHER TRAINING		
TOTAL TIME		

Notes _____

_____

_____

_____

_____

TOTAL DISTANCE

TOTAL DISTANCE

TOTAL DISTANCE

TOTAL DISTANCE

PLANNING CALENDAR

MONDAY ___ / ___ / ___   RESTING HEART RATE _____ WEIGHT _____

DISTANCE _____   TIME _____   PACE/SPLITS _____   INTENSITY FACTOR _____

Notes _____

_____

_____

_____

ACHES AND PAINS _____

Rating	GREAT	VERY GOOD	GOOD	FAIR	POOR	VERY BAD
Nutrition	VEGGIE	FRUIT	GRAIN	MEAT/FISH	NUT/SEED/BEAN	WATER	SWEET	FRIED

TUESDAY ___ / ___ / ___   RESTING HEART RATE _____ WEIGHT _____

DISTANCE _____   TIME _____   PACE/SPLITS _____   INTENSITY FACTOR _____

Notes _____

_____

_____

_____

ACHES AND PAINS _____

Rating	GREAT	VERY GOOD	GOOD	FAIR	POOR	VERY BAD
Nutrition	VEGGIE	FRUIT	GRAIN	MEAT/FISH	NUT/SEED/BEAN	WATER	SWEET	FRIED

degree of pronation increases the risk of any specific injury type. So avoid those overbuilt "motion control" shoes that supposedly limit pronation at the cost of tremendous weight.

WEDNESDAY ___ / ___ / ___   RESTING HEART RATE _____   WEIGHT _____

DISTANCE _____   TIME _____   PACE/SPLITS _____   INTENSITY FACTOR _____

Notes _____

_____

_____

_____

_____

ACHES AND PAINS _____

Rating	GREAT	VERY GOOD		GOOD	FAIR	POOR	VERY BAD
Nutrition	VEGGIE	FRUIT	GRAIN	MEAT/ FISH	NUT/SEED/ BEAN	WATER	SWEET	FRIED

THURSDAY ___ / ___ / ___   RESTING HEART RATE _____   WEIGHT _____

DISTANCE _____   TIME _____   PACE/SPLITS _____   INTENSITY FACTOR _____

Notes _____

_____

_____

_____

ACHES AND PAINS _____

Rating	GREAT	VERY GOOD		GOOD	FAIR	POOR	VERY BAD
Nutrition	VEGGIE	FRUIT	GRAIN	MEAT/ FISH	NUT/SEED/ BEAN	WATER	SWEET	FRIED

FRIDAY ___/___/___

RESTING HEART RATE _____ WEIGHT _____

DISTANCE _____ TIME _____ PACE/SPLITS _____ INTENSITY FACTOR _____

Notes _____

_____

_____

_____

_____

ACHES AND PAINS _____

Rating	GREAT	VERY GOOD		GOOD	FAIR	POOR		VERY BAD
Nutrition	VEGGIE	FRUIT	GRAIN	MEAT/ FISH	NUT/SEED/ BEAN	WATER	SWEET	FRIED

SATURDAY ___/___/___

RESTING HEART RATE _____ WEIGHT _____

DISTANCE _____ TIME _____ PACE/SPLITS _____ INTENSITY FACTOR _____

Notes _____

_____

_____

_____

_____

ACHES AND PAINS _____

Rating	GREAT	VERY GOOD		GOOD	FAIR	POOR		VERY BAD
Nutrition	VEGGIE	FRUIT	GRAIN	MEAT/ FISH	NUT/SEED/ BEAN	WATER	SWEET	FRIED

SUNDAY ___ / ___ / ___

RESTING HEART RATE _____ WEIGHT _____

DISTANCE _____ TIME _____ PACE/SPLITS _____ INTENSITY FACTOR _____

Notes _____

_____

_____

_____

_____

ACHES AND PAINS _____

Rating	GREAT	VERY GOOD	GOOD	FAIR	POOR	VERY BAD

Nutrition	VEGGIE	FRUIT	GRAIN	MEAT/FISH	NUT/SEED/BEAN	WATER	SWEET	FRIED

WEEKLY SUMMARY

AVERAGE INTENSITY FACTOR _____

	WEEKLY TOTAL	YEAR TO DATE
RUN DISTANCE		
RUN TIME		
OTHER TRAINING		
TOTAL TIME		

Notes _____

_____

_____

_____

_____

MONDAY ___ / ___ / ___

RESTING HEART RATE _____ WEIGHT _____

DISTANCE _____ TIME _____ PACE/SPLITS _____ INTENSITY FACTOR _____

Notes _____

_____

_____

_____

ACHES AND PAINS _____

Rating	GREAT	VERY GOOD		GOOD		FAIR	POOR		VERY BAD

Nutrition	VEGGIE	FRUIT	GRAIN	MEAT/ FISH	NUT/SEED/ BEAN	WATER	SWEET	FRIED

TUESDAY ___ / ___ / ___

RESTING HEART RATE _____ WEIGHT _____

DISTANCE _____ TIME _____ PACE/SPLITS _____ INTENSITY FACTOR _____

Notes _____

_____

_____

_____

ACHES AND PAINS _____

Rating	GREAT	VERY GOOD	GOOD	FAIR	POOR	VERY BAD

Nutrition	VEGGIE	FRUIT	GRAIN	MEAT/ FISH	NUT/SEED/ BEAN	WATER	SWEET	FRIED

a half-marathon or marathon. Do it once every 3–4 weeks and look for clear improvement despite equal effort. Spec tests are great workouts in themselves, yet they don't take as much out of you as actual races.

WEDNESDAY ___ / ___ / ___   RESTING HEART RATE ___   WEIGHT ___

DISTANCE ___   TIME ___   PACE/SPLITS ___   INTENSITY FACTOR ___

Notes ___

___

___

___

ACHES AND PAINS ___

Rating	GREAT	VERY GOOD	GOOD	FAIR	POOR	VERY BAD

Nutrition	VEGGIE	FRUIT	GRAIN	MEAT/FISH	NUT/SEED/BEAN	WATER	SWEET	FRIED

THURSDAY ___ / ___ / ___   RESTING HEART RATE ___   WEIGHT ___

DISTANCE ___   TIME ___   PACE/SPLITS ___   INTENSITY FACTOR ___

Notes ___

___

___

___

ACHES AND PAINS ___

Rating	GREAT	VERY GOOD	GOOD	FAIR	POOR	VERY BAD

Nutrition	VEGGIE	FRUIT	GRAIN	MEAT/FISH	NUT/SEED/BEAN	WATER	SWEET	FRIED

FRIDAY ___ / ___ / ___

RESTING HEART RATE _____ WEIGHT _____

DISTANCE _____ TIME _____ PACE/SPLITS _____ INTENSITY FACTOR _____

Notes _____

_____

_____

_____

_____

ACHES AND PAINS _____

Rating	GREAT	VERY GOOD		GOOD		FAIR	POOR	VERY BAD
Nutrition	VEGGIE	FRUIT	GRAIN	MEAT/ FISH	NUT/SEED/ BEAN	WATER	SWEET	FRIED

SATURDAY ___ / ___ / ___

RESTING HEART RATE _____ WEIGHT _____

DISTANCE _____ TIME _____ PACE/SPLITS _____ INTENSITY FACTOR _____

Notes _____

_____

_____

_____

_____

ACHES AND PAINS _____

Rating	GREAT	VERY GOOD		GOOD		FAIR	POOR	VERY BAD
Nutrition	VEGGIE	FRUIT	GRAIN	MEAT/ FISH	NUT/SEED/ BEAN	WATER	SWEET	FRIED

SUNDAY ___/___/___

RESTING HEART RATE _____ WEIGHT _____

DISTANCE _____ TIME _____ PACE/SPLITS _____ INTENSITY FACTOR _____

Notes _____

_____

_____

_____

_____

_____

ACHES AND PAINS _____

Rating	GREAT	VERY GOOD	GOOD	FAIR	POOR	VERY BAD
Nutrition	VEGGIE	FRUIT	GRAIN	MEAT/FISH	NUT/SEED/BEAN	WATER	SWEET	FRIED

WEEKLY SUMMARY

AVERAGE INTENSITY FACTOR _____

	WEEKLY TOTAL	YEAR TO DATE
RUN DISTANCE		
RUN TIME		
OTHER TRAINING		
TOTAL TIME		

Notes _____

_____

_____

_____

_____

MONDAY ___ / ___ / ___   RESTING HEART RATE _____   WEIGHT _____

DISTANCE _____   TIME _____   PACE/SPLITS _____   INTENSITY FACTOR _____

Notes _____

_____

_____

_____

ACHES AND PAINS _____

Rating	GREAT	VERY GOOD		GOOD		FAIR	POOR	VERY BAD
Nutrition	VEGGIE	FRUIT	GRAIN	MEAT/ FISH	NUT/SEED/ BEAN	WATER	SWEET	FRIED

TUESDAY ___ / ___ / ___   RESTING HEART RATE _____   WEIGHT _____

DISTANCE _____   TIME _____   PACE/SPLITS _____   INTENSITY FACTOR _____

Notes _____

_____

_____

_____

ACHES AND PAINS _____

Rating	GREAT	VERY GOOD		GOOD		FAIR	POOR	VERY BAD
Nutrition	VEGGIE	FRUIT	GRAIN	MEAT/ FISH	NUT/SEED/ BEAN	WATER	SWEET	FRIED

their performance in the next hard session. Take a page from the Africans' book and take it really easy on your easy days.

WEDNESDAY ___/___/___ RESTING HEART RATE _____ WEIGHT _____

DISTANCE _____ TIME _____ PACE/SPLITS _____ INTENSITY FACTOR _____

Notes _____

_____

_____

_____

ACHES AND PAINS _____

Rating	GREAT	VERY GOOD		GOOD	FAIR	POOR	VERY BAD
Nutrition	VEGGIE	FRUIT	GRAIN	MEAT/ FISH	NUT/SEED/ BEAN	WATER	SWEET	FRIED

THURSDAY ___/___/___ RESTING HEART RATE _____ WEIGHT _____

DISTANCE _____ TIME _____ PACE/SPLITS _____ INTENSITY FACTOR _____

Notes _____

_____

_____

_____

ACHES AND PAINS _____

Rating	GREAT	VERY GOOD		GOOD	FAIR	POOR	VERY BAD
Nutrition	VEGGIE	FRUIT	GRAIN	MEAT/ FISH	NUT/SEED/ BEAN	WATER	SWEET	FRIED

FRIDAY ____/____/____

RESTING HEART RATE _____ WEIGHT _____

DISTANCE _____ TIME _____ PACE/SPLITS _____ INTENSITY FACTOR _____

Notes _____

_____

_____

_____

_____

ACHES AND PAINS _____

Rating	GREAT		VERY GOOD		GOOD		FAIR		POOR		VERY BAD
Nutrition	VEGGIE	FRUIT	GRAIN	MEAT/FISH	NUT/SEED/BEAN	WATER	SWEET	FRIED

SATURDAY ____/____/____

RESTING HEART RATE _____ WEIGHT _____

DISTANCE _____ TIME _____ PACE/SPLITS _____ INTENSITY FACTOR _____

Notes _____

_____

_____

_____

_____

ACHES AND PAINS _____

Rating	GREAT		VERY GOOD		GOOD		FAIR		POOR		VERY BAD
Nutrition	VEGGIE	FRUIT	GRAIN	MEAT/FISH	NUT/SEED/BEAN	WATER	SWEET	FRIED

SUNDAY ___ / ___ / ___   RESTING HEART RATE _____ WEIGHT _____

DISTANCE _____   TIME _____   PACE/SPLITS _____   INTENSITY FACTOR _____

Notes _____

_____

_____

_____

_____

ACHES AND PAINS _____

Rating	GREAT	VERY GOOD	GOOD	FAIR	POOR	VERY BAD

Nutrition	VEGGIE	FRUIT	GRAIN	MEAT/ FISH	NUT/SEED/ BEAN	WATER	SWEET	FRIED

WEEKLY SUMMARY   AVERAGE INTENSITY FACTOR _____

	WEEKLY TOTAL	YEAR TO DATE
RUN DISTANCE		
RUN TIME		
OTHER TRAINING		
TOTAL TIME		

Notes _____

_____

_____

_____

_____

MONDAY ___ / ___ / ___   RESTING HEART RATE _____ WEIGHT _____

DISTANCE _____   TIME _____   PACE/SPLITS _____   INTENSITY FACTOR _____

Notes _____

_____

_____

_____

ACHES AND PAINS _____

Rating	GREAT		VERY GOOD		GOOD		FAIR		POOR		VERY BAD

Nutrition	VEGGIE	FRUIT	GRAIN	MEAT/FISH	NUT/SEED/BEAN	WATER	SWEET	FRIED

TUESDAY ___ / ___ / ___   RESTING HEART RATE _____ WEIGHT _____

DISTANCE _____   TIME _____   PACE/SPLITS _____   INTENSITY FACTOR _____

Notes _____

_____

_____

_____

ACHES AND PAINS _____

Rating	GREAT		VERY GOOD		GOOD		FAIR		POOR		VERY BAD

Nutrition	VEGGIE	FRUIT	GRAIN	MEAT/FISH	NUT/SEED/BEAN	WATER	SWEET	FRIED

running. More and more major running events are streamed live on the Internet, making it ever easier to be an active running fan.

WEDNESDAY ___/___/___   RESTING HEART RATE _____   WEIGHT _____

DISTANCE _____   TIME _____   PACE/SPLITS _____   INTENSITY FACTOR _____

Notes _____

_____

_____

_____

ACHES AND PAINS _____

Rating	GREAT	VERY GOOD		GOOD	FAIR		POOR	VERY BAD
Nutrition	VEGGIE	FRUIT	GRAIN	MEAT/ FISH	NUT/SEED/ BEAN	WATER	SWEET	FRIED

THURSDAY ___/___/___   RESTING HEART RATE _____   WEIGHT _____

DISTANCE _____   TIME _____   PACE/SPLITS _____   INTENSITY FACTOR _____

Notes _____

_____

_____

_____

ACHES AND PAINS _____

Rating	GREAT	VERY GOOD		GOOD	FAIR		POOR	VERY BAD
Nutrition	VEGGIE	FRUIT	GRAIN	MEAT/ FISH	NUT/SEED/ BEAN	WATER	SWEET	FRIED

FRIDAY ___ / ___ / ___

RESTING HEART RATE _____ WEIGHT _____

DISTANCE _____   TIME _____   PACE/SPLITS _____   INTENSITY FACTOR _____

Notes _____

_____

_____

_____

_____

ACHES AND PAINS _____

Rating	GREAT	VERY GOOD		GOOD	FAIR		POOR	VERY BAD
Nutrition	VEGGIE	FRUIT	GRAIN	MEAT/ FISH	NUT/SEED/ BEAN	WATER	SWEET	FRIED

SATURDAY ___ / ___ / ___

RESTING HEART RATE _____ WEIGHT _____

DISTANCE _____   TIME _____   PACE/SPLITS _____   INTENSITY FACTOR _____

Notes _____

_____

_____

_____

_____

ACHES AND PAINS _____

Rating	GREAT	VERY GOOD		GOOD	FAIR		POOR	VERY BAD
Nutrition	VEGGIE	FRUIT	GRAIN	MEAT/ FISH	NUT/SEED/ BEAN	WATER	SWEET	FRIED

SUNDAY ___ / ___ / ___

RESTING HEART RATE _____ WEIGHT _____

DISTANCE _____ TIME _____ PACE/SPLITS _____ INTENSITY FACTOR _____

Notes _____

_____

_____

_____

_____

ACHES AND PAINS _____

Rating	GREAT	VERY GOOD		GOOD		FAIR		POOR		VERY BAD
Nutrition	VEGGIE	FRUIT	GRAIN	MEAT/ FISH	NUT/SEED/ BEAN	WATER	SWEET	FRIED		

WEEKLY SUMMARY

AVERAGE INTENSITY FACTOR _____

	WEEKLY TOTAL	YEAR TO DATE
RUN DISTANCE		
RUN TIME		
OTHER TRAINING		
TOTAL TIME		

Notes _____

_____

_____

_____

_____

MONDAY	TUESDAY	WEDNESDAY	THURSDAY

TOTAL DISTANCE

TOTAL DISTANCE

TOTAL DISTANCE

TOTAL DISTANCE

PLANNING CALENDAR

MONDAY ___ / ___ / ___   RESTING HEART RATE ___   WEIGHT ___

DISTANCE ___   TIME ___   PACE/SPLITS ___   INTENSITY FACTOR ___

Notes ___

___

___

___

ACHES AND PAINS ___

Rating	GREAT	VERY GOOD		GOOD	FAIR		POOR	VERY BAD
Nutrition	VEGGIE	FRUIT	GRAIN	MEAT/ FISH	NUT/SEED/ BEAN	WATER	SWEET	FRIED

TUESDAY ___ / ___ / ___   RESTING HEART RATE ___   WEIGHT ___

DISTANCE ___   TIME ___   PACE/SPLITS ___   INTENSITY FACTOR ___

Notes ___

___

___

___

ACHES AND PAINS ___

Rating	GREAT	VERY GOOD		GOOD	FAIR		POOR	VERY BAD
Nutrition	VEGGIE	FRUIT	GRAIN	MEAT/ FISH	NUT/SEED/ BEAN	WATER	SWEET	FRIED

your diet for a week before racing. Also, caffeine pills work better than coffee. Take 5–6 mg of caffeine per kg (2.25–2.75 mg per lb.) of body weight 1 hour before your race starts.

WEDNESDAY ___ / ___ / ___   RESTING HEART RATE _____   WEIGHT _____

DISTANCE _____   TIME _____   PACE/SPLITS _____   INTENSITY FACTOR _____

Notes _____

_____

_____

_____

ACHES AND PAINS _____

Rating	GREAT	VERY GOOD		GOOD		FAIR	POOR		VERY BAD
Nutrition	VEGGIE	FRUIT	GRAIN	MEAT/ FISH	NUT/SEED/ BEAN	WATER		SWEET	FRIED

THURSDAY ___ / ___ / ___   RESTING HEART RATE _____   WEIGHT _____

DISTANCE _____   TIME _____   PACE/SPLITS _____   INTENSITY FACTOR _____

Notes _____

_____

_____

_____

ACHES AND PAINS _____

Rating	GREAT	VERY GOOD		GOOD		FAIR	POOR		VERY BAD
Nutrition	VEGGIE	FRUIT	GRAIN	MEAT/ FISH	NUT/SEED/ BEAN	WATER		SWEET	FRIED

FRIDAY ___ / ___ / ___

RESTING HEART RATE _____ WEIGHT _____

DISTANCE _____ TIME _____ PACE/SPLITS _____ INTENSITY FACTOR _____

Notes _____

_____

_____

_____

_____

ACHES AND PAINS _____

Rating	GREAT	VERY GOOD		GOOD	FAIR		POOR		VERY BAD
Nutrition	VEGGIE	FRUIT	GRAIN	MEAT/ FISH	NUT/SEED/ BEAN	WATER	SWEET		FRIED

SATURDAY ___ / ___ / ___

RESTING HEART RATE _____ WEIGHT _____

DISTANCE _____ TIME _____ PACE/SPLITS _____ INTENSITY FACTOR _____

Notes _____

_____

_____

_____

_____

ACHES AND PAINS _____

Rating	GREAT	VERY GOOD		GOOD	FAIR		POOR		VERY BAD
Nutrition	VEGGIE	FRUIT	GRAIN	MEAT/ FISH	NUT/SEED/ BEAN	WATER	SWEET		FRIED

SUNDAY ___ / ___ / ___

RESTING HEART RATE _____ WEIGHT _____

DISTANCE _____ TIME _____ PACE/SPLITS _____ INTENSITY FACTOR _____

Notes _____

_____

_____

_____

_____

ACHES AND PAINS _____

Rating	GREAT	VERY GOOD		GOOD		FAIR		POOR		VERY BAD
Nutrition	VEGGIE	FRUIT	GRAIN	MEAT/FISH	NUT/SEED/BEAN	WATER	SWEET	FRIED

WEEKLY SUMMARY

AVERAGE INTENSITY FACTOR _____

	WEEKLY TOTAL	YEAR TO DATE
RUN DISTANCE		
RUN TIME		
OTHER TRAINING		
TOTAL TIME		

Notes _____

_____

_____

_____

_____

MONDAY ____ / ____ / ____   RESTING HEART RATE _____ WEIGHT _____

DISTANCE _____   TIME _____   PACE/SPLITS _____   INTENSITY FACTOR _____

Notes _____

_____

_____

_____

ACHES AND PAINS _____

Rating GREAT   VERY GOOD   GOOD   FAIR   POOR   VERY BAD

Nutrition	VEGGIE	FRUIT	GRAIN	MEAT/ FISH	NUT/SEED/ BEAN	WATER	SWEET	FRIED

TUESDAY ____ / ____ / ____   RESTING HEART RATE _____ WEIGHT _____

DISTANCE _____   TIME _____   PACE/SPLITS _____   INTENSITY FACTOR _____

Notes _____

_____

_____

_____

ACHES AND PAINS _____

Rating GREAT   VERY GOOD   GOOD   FAIR   POOR   VERY BAD

Nutrition	VEGGIE	FRUIT	GRAIN	MEAT/ FISH	NUT/SEED/ BEAN	WATER	SWEET	FRIED

WEDNESDAY ___/___/___   RESTING HEART RATE _____ WEIGHT _____

DISTANCE _____   TIME _____   PACE/SPLITS _____   INTENSITY FACTOR _____

Notes _____

_____

_____

_____

ACHES AND PAINS _____

Rating	GREAT	VERY GOOD	GOOD	FAIR	POOR	VERY BAD

Nutrition	VEGGIE	FRUIT	GRAIN	MEAT/FISH	NUT/SEED/BEAN	WATER	SWEET	FRIED

THURSDAY ___/___/___   RESTING HEART RATE _____ WEIGHT _____

DISTANCE _____   TIME _____   PACE/SPLITS _____   INTENSITY FACTOR _____

Notes _____

_____

_____

_____

ACHES AND PAINS _____

Rating	GREAT	VERY GOOD	GOOD	FAIR	POOR	VERY BAD

Nutrition	VEGGIE	FRUIT	GRAIN	MEAT/FISH	NUT/SEED/BEAN	WATER	SWEET	FRIED

FRIDAY ___ / ___ / ___

RESTING HEART RATE _____ WEIGHT _____

DISTANCE _____ TIME _____ PACE/SPLITS _____ INTENSITY FACTOR _____

Notes _____

_____

_____

_____

_____

ACHES AND PAINS _____

Rating	GREAT	VERY GOOD	GOOD	FAIR	POOR	VERY BAD
Nutrition	VEGGIE	FRUIT	GRAIN	MEAT/FISH	NUT/SEED/BEAN	WATER	SWEET	FRIED

SATURDAY ___ / ___ / ___

RESTING HEART RATE _____ WEIGHT _____

DISTANCE _____ TIME _____ PACE/SPLITS _____ INTENSITY FACTOR _____

Notes _____

_____

_____

_____

_____

ACHES AND PAINS _____

Rating	GREAT	VERY GOOD	GOOD	FAIR	POOR	VERY BAD
Nutrition	VEGGIE	FRUIT	GRAIN	MEAT/FISH	NUT/SEED/BEAN	WATER	SWEET	FRIED

SUNDAY ___/___/___

RESTING HEART RATE _____ WEIGHT _____

DISTANCE _____ TIME _____ PACE/SPLITS _____ INTENSITY FACTOR _____

Notes _____

_____

_____

_____

_____

ACHES AND PAINS _____

Rating | GREAT | VERY GOOD | GOOD | FAIR | POOR | VERY BAD

Nutrition	VEGGIE	FRUIT	GRAIN	MEAT/FISH	NUT/SEED/BEAN	WATER	SWEET	FRIED

WEEKLY SUMMARY

AVERAGE INTENSITY FACTOR _____

	WEEKLY TOTAL	YEAR TO DATE
RUN DISTANCE		
RUN TIME		
OTHER TRAINING		
TOTAL TIME		

Notes _____

_____

_____

_____

_____

MONDAY ___ / ___ / ___   RESTING HEART RATE _____ WEIGHT _____

DISTANCE _____   TIME _____   PACE/SPLITS _____   INTENSITY FACTOR _____

Notes _____

_____

_____

_____

ACHES AND PAINS _____

Rating	GREAT	VERY GOOD	GOOD	FAIR	POOR	VERY BAD

Nutrition	VEGGIE	FRUIT	GRAIN	MEAT/ FISH	NUT/SEED/ BEAN	WATER	SWEET	FRIED

TUESDAY ___ / ___ / ___   RESTING HEART RATE _____ WEIGHT _____

DISTANCE _____   TIME _____   PACE/SPLITS _____   INTENSITY FACTOR _____

Notes _____

_____

_____

_____

ACHES AND PAINS _____

Rating	GREAT	VERY GOOD	GOOD	FAIR	POOR	VERY BAD

Nutrition	VEGGIE	FRUIT	GRAIN	MEAT/ FISH	NUT/SEED/ BEAN	WATER	SWEET	FRIED

forward on your left leg for 20 paces. Do this once a week. As single-leg running gets easier, build up to 30 hops per leg and then begin doing the drill twice during your run—once near the beginning and again toward the end.

WEDNESDAY ___ / ___ / ___   RESTING HEART RATE ___   WEIGHT ___

DISTANCE ___   TIME ___   PACE/SPLITS ___   INTENSITY FACTOR ___

Notes _____

_____

_____

_____

ACHES AND PAINS _____

Rating	GREAT	VERY GOOD		GOOD	FAIR		POOR	VERY BAD

Nutrition	VEGGIE	FRUIT	GRAIN	MEAT/FISH	NUT/SEED/BEAN	WATER	SWEET	FRIED

THURSDAY ___ / ___ / ___   RESTING HEART RATE ___   WEIGHT ___

DISTANCE ___   TIME ___   PACE/SPLITS ___   INTENSITY FACTOR ___

Notes _____

_____

_____

_____

ACHES AND PAINS _____

Rating	GREAT	VERY GOOD		GOOD	FAIR		POOR	VERY BAD

Nutrition	VEGGIE	FRUIT	GRAIN	MEAT/FISH	NUT/SEED/BEAN	WATER	SWEET	FRIED

FRIDAY ___ / ___ / ___

RESTING HEART RATE _____ WEIGHT _____

DISTANCE _____ TIME _____ PACE/SPLITS _____ INTENSITY FACTOR _____

Notes _____

_____

_____

_____

_____

ACHES AND PAINS _____

Rating	GREAT	VERY GOOD		GOOD	FAIR		POOR	VERY BAD

Nutrition	VEGGIE	FRUIT	GRAIN	MEAT/FISH	NUT/SEED/BEAN	WATER	SWEET	FRIED

SATURDAY ___ / ___ / ___

RESTING HEART RATE _____ WEIGHT _____

DISTANCE _____ TIME _____ PACE/SPLITS _____ INTENSITY FACTOR _____

Notes _____

_____

_____

_____

_____

ACHES AND PAINS _____

Rating	GREAT	VERY GOOD		GOOD	FAIR		POOR	VERY BAD

Nutrition	VEGGIE	FRUIT	GRAIN	MEAT/FISH	NUT/SEED/BEAN	WATER	SWEET	FRIED

SUNDAY ___ / ___ / ___

RESTING HEART RATE _____ WEIGHT _____

DISTANCE _____ TIME _____ PACE/SPLITS _____ INTENSITY FACTOR _____

Notes _____

_____

_____

_____

_____

_____

ACHES AND PAINS _____

Rating	GREAT	VERY GOOD		GOOD	FAIR		POOR	VERY BAD
Nutrition	VEGGIE	FRUIT	GRAIN	MEAT/ FISH	NUT/SEED/ BEAN	WATER	SWEET	FRIED

WEEKLY SUMMARY

AVERAGE INTENSITY FACTOR _____

	WEEKLY TOTAL	YEAR TO DATE
RUN DISTANCE		
RUN TIME		
OTHER TRAINING		
TOTAL TIME		

Notes _____

_____

_____

_____

_____

MONDAY ___ / ___ / ___   RESTING HEART RATE _____ WEIGHT _____

DISTANCE _____   TIME _____   PACE/SPLITS _____   INTENSITY FACTOR _____

Notes _____

_____

_____

_____

ACHES AND PAINS _____

Rating   GREAT   VERY GOOD   GOOD   FAIR   POOR   VERY BAD

Nutrition   VEGGIE   FRUIT   GRAIN   MEAT/FISH   NUT/SEED/BEAN   WATER   SWEET   FRIED

TUESDAY ___ / ___ / ___   RESTING HEART RATE _____ WEIGHT _____

DISTANCE _____   TIME _____   PACE/SPLITS _____   INTENSITY FACTOR _____

Notes _____

_____

_____

_____

ACHES AND PAINS _____

Rating   GREAT   VERY GOOD   GOOD   FAIR   POOR   VERY BAD

Nutrition   VEGGIE   FRUIT   GRAIN   MEAT/FISH   NUT/SEED/BEAN   WATER   SWEET   FRIED

the road behind you with each foot. This proprioceptive cue will encourage you to begin retracting your leg before your foot lands so that your foot lands underneath your body, as it should, rather than ahead of it.

WEDNESDAY ___ / ___ / ___   RESTING HEART RATE ___   WEIGHT ___

DISTANCE ___   TIME ___   PACE/SPLITS ___   INTENSITY FACTOR ___

Notes ___

___

___

___

ACHES AND PAINS ___

Rating	GREAT	VERY GOOD	GOOD	FAIR	POOR	VERY BAD

Nutrition	VEGGIE	FRUIT	GRAIN	MEAT/FISH	NUT/SEED/BEAN	WATER	SWEET	FRIED

THURSDAY ___ / ___ / ___   RESTING HEART RATE ___   WEIGHT ___

DISTANCE ___   TIME ___   PACE/SPLITS ___   INTENSITY FACTOR ___

Notes ___

___

___

___

ACHES AND PAINS ___

Rating	GREAT	VERY GOOD	GOOD	FAIR	POOR	VERY BAD

Nutrition	VEGGIE	FRUIT	GRAIN	MEAT/FISH	NUT/SEED/BEAN	WATER	SWEET	FRIED

FRIDAY ___ / ___ / ___

RESTING HEART RATE _____ WEIGHT _____

DISTANCE _____ TIME _____ PACE/SPLITS _____ INTENSITY FACTOR _____

Notes _____

_____

_____

_____

_____

ACHES AND PAINS _____

Rating	GREAT	VERY GOOD		GOOD	FAIR	POOR		VERY BAD
Nutrition	VEGGIE	FRUIT	GRAIN	MEAT/ FISH	NUT/SEED/ BEAN	WATER	SWEET	FRIED

SATURDAY ___ / ___ / ___

RESTING HEART RATE _____ WEIGHT _____

DISTANCE _____ TIME _____ PACE/SPLITS _____ INTENSITY FACTOR _____

Notes _____

_____

_____

_____

_____

ACHES AND PAINS _____

Rating	GREAT	VERY GOOD		GOOD	FAIR	POOR		VERY BAD
Nutrition	VEGGIE	FRUIT	GRAIN	MEAT/ FISH	NUT/SEED/ BEAN	WATER	SWEET	FRIED

SUNDAY ___ / ___ / ___   RESTING HEART RATE _____ WEIGHT _____

DISTANCE _____   TIME _____   PACE/SPLITS _____   INTENSITY FACTOR _____

Notes _____

_____

_____

_____

_____

_____

ACHES AND PAINS _____

Rating	GREAT	VERY GOOD		GOOD	FAIR	POOR	VERY BAD

Nutrition	VEGGIE	FRUIT	GRAIN	MEAT/ FISH	NUT/SEED/ BEAN	WATER	SWEET	FRIED

WEEKLY SUMMARY   AVERAGE INTENSITY FACTOR _____

	WEEKLY TOTAL	YEAR TO DATE
RUN DISTANCE		
RUN TIME		
OTHER TRAINING		
TOTAL TIME		

Notes _____

_____

_____

_____

_____

_____

MONDAY	TUESDAY	WEDNESDAY	THURSDAY

TOTAL DISTANCE

TOTAL DISTANCE

TOTAL DISTANCE

TOTAL DISTANCE

PLANNING CALENDAR

MONDAY ___ / ___ / ___   RESTING HEART RATE _____ WEIGHT _____

DISTANCE _____   TIME _____   PACE/SPLITS _____   INTENSITY FACTOR _____

Notes _____

_____

_____

_____

ACHES AND PAINS _____

Rating	GREAT	VERY GOOD	GOOD	FAIR	POOR	VERY BAD
Nutrition	VEGGIE	FRUIT	GRAIN	MEAT/FISH	NUT/SEED/BEAN	WATER	SWEET	FRIED

TUESDAY ___ / ___ / ___   RESTING HEART RATE _____ WEIGHT _____

DISTANCE _____   TIME _____   PACE/SPLITS _____   INTENSITY FACTOR _____

Notes _____

_____

_____

_____

ACHES AND PAINS _____

Rating	GREAT	VERY GOOD	GOOD	FAIR	POOR	VERY BAD
Nutrition	VEGGIE	FRUIT	GRAIN	MEAT/FISH	NUT/SEED/BEAN	WATER	SWEET	FRIED

*your fitness a quick boost without overtaxing your body. For example, warm up
and then run 4 x 800 meters at 3000-meter race pace with 400-meter jogging
recoveries between intervals.*

WEDNESDAY ____ / ____ / ____   RESTING HEART RATE _____ WEIGHT _____

DISTANCE _____   TIME _____   PACE/SPLITS _____   INTENSITY FACTOR _____

Notes _____

_____

_____

_____

ACHES AND PAINS _____

Rating	GREAT	VERY GOOD		GOOD	FAIR		POOR	VERY BAD
Nutrition	VEGGIE	FRUIT	GRAIN	MEAT/ FISH	NUT/SEED/ BEAN	WATER	SWEET	FRIED

THURSDAY ____ / ____ / ____   RESTING HEART RATE _____ WEIGHT _____

DISTANCE _____   TIME _____   PACE/SPLITS _____   INTENSITY FACTOR _____

Notes _____

_____

_____

_____

ACHES AND PAINS _____

Rating	GREAT	VERY GOOD		GOOD	FAIR		POOR	VERY BAD
Nutrition	VEGGIE	FRUIT	GRAIN	MEAT/ FISH	NUT/SEED/ BEAN	WATER	SWEET	FRIED

FRIDAY ___ / ___ / ___

RESTING HEART RATE _____ WEIGHT _____

DISTANCE _____ TIME _____ PACE/SPLITS _____ INTENSITY FACTOR _____

Notes _____

_____

_____

_____

_____

ACHES AND PAINS _____

Rating	GREAT	VERY GOOD	GOOD	FAIR	POOR	VERY BAD

Nutrition	VEGGIE	FRUIT	GRAIN	MEAT/FISH	NUT/SEED/BEAN	WATER	SWEET	FRIED

SATURDAY ___ / ___ / ___

RESTING HEART RATE _____ WEIGHT _____

DISTANCE _____ TIME _____ PACE/SPLITS _____ INTENSITY FACTOR _____

Notes _____

_____

_____

_____

_____

ACHES AND PAINS _____

Rating	GREAT	VERY GOOD	GOOD	FAIR	POOR	VERY BAD

Nutrition	VEGGIE	FRUIT	GRAIN	MEAT/FISH	NUT/SEED/BEAN	WATER	SWEET	FRIED

SUNDAY ____ / ____ / ____

RESTING HEART RATE _____ WEIGHT _____

DISTANCE _____ TIME _____ PACE/SPLITS _____ INTENSITY FACTOR _____

Notes _____

_____

_____

_____

_____

ACHES AND PAINS _____

Rating | GREAT | VERY GOOD | GOOD | FAIR | POOR | VERY BAD

| Nutrition | VEGGIE | FRUIT | GRAIN | MEAT/FISH | NUT/SEED/BEAN | WATER | SWEET | FRIED |

WEEKLY SUMMARY

AVERAGE INTENSITY FACTOR _____

	WEEKLY TOTAL	YEAR TO DATE
RUN DISTANCE		
RUN TIME		
OTHER TRAINING		
TOTAL TIME		

Notes _____

_____

_____

_____

_____

MONDAY ___ / ___ / ___   RESTING HEART RATE _____ WEIGHT _____

DISTANCE _____   TIME _____   PACE/SPLITS _____   INTENSITY FACTOR _____

Notes _____

_____

_____

_____

ACHES AND PAINS _____

Rating	GREAT	VERY GOOD		GOOD	FAIR	POOR	VERY BAD
Nutrition	VEGGIE	FRUIT	GRAIN	MEAT/FISH	NUT/SEED/BEAN	WATER	SWEET	FRIED

TUESDAY ___ / ___ / ___   RESTING HEART RATE _____ WEIGHT _____

DISTANCE _____   TIME _____   PACE/SPLITS _____   INTENSITY FACTOR _____

Notes _____

_____

_____

_____

ACHES AND PAINS _____

Rating	GREAT	VERY GOOD		GOOD	FAIR	POOR	VERY BAD
Nutrition	VEGGIE	FRUIT	GRAIN	MEAT/FISH	NUT/SEED/BEAN	WATER	SWEET	FRIED

I'm struggling with—it reduces my suffering just a bit. Put some thought into determining which mental games work best for you, and actively call on them whenever you need them.

WEDNESDAY ___/___/___   RESTING HEART RATE _____   WEIGHT _____

DISTANCE _____   TIME _____   PACE/SPLITS _____   INTENSITY FACTOR _____

Notes _____

_____

_____

_____

CHES AND PAINS _____

Rating	GREAT	VERY GOOD		GOOD		FAIR		POOR	VERY BAD
Nutrition	VEGGIE	FRUIT	GRAIN	MEAT/ FISH	NUT/SEED/ BEAN	WATER		SWEET	FRIED

THURSDAY ___/___/___   RESTING HEART RATE _____   WEIGHT _____

DISTANCE _____   TIME _____   PACE/SPLITS _____   INTENSITY FACTOR _____

Notes _____

_____

_____

_____

CHES AND PAINS _____

Rating	GREAT	VERY GOOD		GOOD		FAIR		POOR	VERY BAD
Nutrition	VEGGIE	FRUIT	GRAIN	MEAT/ FISH	NUT/SEED/ BEAN	WATER		SWEET	FRIED

FRIDAY ___ / ___ / ___

RESTING HEART RATE _____ WEIGHT _____

DISTANCE _____ TIME _____ PACE/SPLITS _____ INTENSITY FACTOR _____

Notes _____

_____

_____

_____

_____

ACHES AND PAINS _____

Rating	GREAT	VERY GOOD	GOOD	FAIR	POOR	VERY BAD

Nutrition	VEGGIE	FRUIT	GRAIN	MEAT/FISH	NUT/SEED/BEAN	WATER	SWEET	FRIED

SATURDAY ___ / ___ / ___

RESTING HEART RATE _____ WEIGHT _____

DISTANCE _____ TIME _____ PACE/SPLITS _____ INTENSITY FACTOR _____

Notes _____

_____

_____

_____

_____

ACHES AND PAINS _____

Rating	GREAT	VERY GOOD	GOOD	FAIR	POOR	VERY BAD

Nutrition	VEGGIE	FRUIT	GRAIN	MEAT/FISH	NUT/SEED/BEAN	WATER	SWEET	FRIED

SUNDAY _____ / _____ / _____

RESTING HEART RATE _____ WEIGHT _____

DISTANCE _____ TIME _____ PACE/SPLITS _____ INTENSITY FACTOR _____

Notes

_____

_____

_____

_____

_____

_____

ACHES AND PAINS _____

Rating

| GREAT | VERY GOOD | GOOD | FAIR | POOR | VERY BAD |

Nutrition

| VEGGIE | FRUIT | GRAIN | MEAT/ FISH | NUT/SEED/ BEAN | WATER | SWEET | FRIED |

WEEKLY SUMMARY

AVERAGE INTENSITY FACTOR _____

	WEEKLY TOTAL	YEAR TO DATE
RUN DISTANCE		
RUN TIME		
OTHER TRAINING		
TOTAL TIME		

Notes

_____

_____

_____

_____

_____

MONDAY ___ / ___ / ___   RESTING HEART RATE _____ WEIGHT _____

DISTANCE _____   TIME _____   PACE/SPLITS _____   INTENSITY FACTOR _____

Notes _____

_____

_____

_____

ACHES AND PAINS _____

Rating	GREAT	VERY GOOD		GOOD	FAIR		POOR	VERY BAD

Nutrition	VEGGIE	FRUIT	GRAIN	MEAT/ FISH	NUT/SEED/ BEAN	WATER	SWEET	FRIED

TUESDAY ___ / ___ / ___   RESTING HEART RATE _____ WEIGHT _____

DISTANCE _____   TIME _____   PACE/SPLITS _____   INTENSITY FACTOR _____

Notes _____

_____

_____

_____

ACHES AND PAINS _____

Rating	GREAT	VERY GOOD		GOOD	FAIR		POOR	VERY BAD

Nutrition	VEGGIE	FRUIT	GRAIN	MEAT/ FISH	NUT/SEED/ BEAN	WATER	SWEET	FRIED

Progression runs make excellent moderate runs. In them, you run a few miles at an easy pace and then the last mile or two at a moderately hard pace. Putting the hard part at the end helps ensure that you don't overdo it.

WEDNESDAY ___ / ___ / ___   RESTING HEART RATE ___   WEIGHT ___

DISTANCE ___   TIME ___   PACE/SPLITS ___   INTENSITY FACTOR ___

Notes _____

_____

_____

_____

ACHES AND PAINS _____

Rating	GREAT	VERY GOOD		GOOD	FAIR	POOR	VERY BAD
Nutrition	VEGGIE	FRUIT	GRAIN	MEAT/FISH	NUT/SEED/BEAN	WATER	SWEET	FRIED

THURSDAY ___ / ___   RESTING HEART RATE ___   WEIGHT ___

DISTANCE ___   TIME ___   PACE/SPLITS ___   INTENSITY FACTOR ___

Notes _____

_____

_____

_____

ACHES AND PAINS _____

Rating	GREAT	VERY GOOD		GOOD	FAIR	POOR	VERY BAD
Nutrition	VEGGIE	FRUIT	GRAIN	MEAT/FISH	NUT/SEED/BEAN	WATER	SWEET	FRIED

FRIDAY ___ / ___ / ___

RESTING HEART RATE _____ WEIGHT _____

DISTANCE _____ TIME _____ PACE/SPLITS _____ INTENSITY FACTOR _____

Notes _____

_____

_____

_____

_____

ACHES AND PAINS _____

Rating	GREAT		VERY GOOD		GOOD		FAIR		POOR		VERY BAD
Nutrition	VEGGIE	FRUIT	GRAIN	MEAT/ FISH	NUT/SEED/ BEAN	WATER	SWEET	FRIED			

SATURDAY ___ / ___ / ___

RESTING HEART RATE _____ WEIGHT _____

DISTANCE _____ TIME _____ PACE/SPLITS _____ INTENSITY FACTOR _____

Notes _____

_____

_____

_____

_____

ACHES AND PAINS _____

Rating	GREAT		VERY GOOD		GOOD		FAIR		POOR		VERY BAD
Nutrition	VEGGIE	FRUIT	GRAIN	MEAT/ FISH	NUT/SEED/ BEAN	WATER	SWEET	FRIED			

SUNDAY ___ / ___ / ___

RESTING HEART RATE _____ WEIGHT _____

DISTANCE _____ TIME _____ PACE/SPLITS _____ INTENSITY FACTOR _____

Notes _____

_____

_____

_____

_____

_____

ACHES AND PAINS _____

Rating

GREAT	VERY GOOD	GOOD	FAIR	POOR	VERY BAD

Nutrition

VEGGIE	FRUIT	GRAIN	MEAT/ FISH	NUT/SEED/ BEAN	WATER	SWEET	FRIED

WEEKLY SUMMARY

AVERAGE INTENSITY FACTOR _____

	WEEKLY TOTAL	YEAR TO DATE
RUN DISTANCE		
RUN TIME		
OTHER TRAINING		
TOTAL TIME		

Notes _____

_____

_____

_____

_____

MONDAY _____ / _____ / _____   RESTING HEART RATE _____ WEIGHT _____

DISTANCE _____   TIME _____   PACE/SPLITS _____   INTENSITY FACTOR _____

Notes _____

_____

_____

_____

ACHES AND PAINS _____

Rating   GREAT   VERY GOOD   GOOD   FAIR   POOR   VERY BAD

Nutrition   VEGGIE   FRUIT   GRAIN   MEAT/ FISH   NUT/SEED/ BEAN   WATER   SWEET   FRIED

TUESDAY _____ / _____ / _____   RESTING HEART RATE _____ WEIGHT _____

DISTANCE _____   TIME _____   PACE/SPLITS _____   INTENSITY FACTOR _____

Notes _____

_____

_____

_____

ACHES AND PAINS _____

Rating   GREAT   VERY GOOD   GOOD   FAIR   POOR   VERY BAD

Nutrition   VEGGIE   FRUIT   GRAIN   MEAT/ FISH   NUT/SEED/ BEAN   WATER   SWEET   FRIED

One way to do so is to rate your mental toughness after each hard workout and race. This will encourage you to dig deeper.

WEDNESDAY ___ / ___ / ___   RESTING HEART RATE _____ WEIGHT _____

DISTANCE _____   TIME _____   PACE/SPLITS _____   INTENSITY FACTOR _____

Notes _____

_____

_____

_____

ACHES AND PAINS _____

Rating	GREAT	VERY GOOD	GOOD	FAIR	POOR	VERY BAD

Nutrition	VEGGIE	FRUIT	GRAIN	MEAT/FISH	NUT/SEED/BEAN	WATER	SWEET	FRIED

THURSDAY ___ / ___ / ___   RESTING HEART RATE _____ WEIGHT _____

DISTANCE _____   TIME _____   PACE/SPLITS _____   INTENSITY FACTOR _____

Notes _____

_____

_____

_____

ACHES AND PAINS _____

Rating	GREAT	VERY GOOD	GOOD	FAIR	POOR	VERY BAD

Nutrition	VEGGIE	FRUIT	GRAIN	MEAT/FISH	NUT/SEED/BEAN	WATER	SWEET	FRIED

FRIDAY ____ / ____ / ____

RESTING HEART RATE _____ WEIGHT _____

DISTANCE _____   TIME _____   PACE/SPLITS _____   INTENSITY FACTOR _____

Notes _____

_____

_____

_____

_____

_____

ACHES AND PAINS _____

Rating	GREAT	VERY GOOD	GOOD	FAIR	POOR	VERY BAD

Nutrition	VEGGIE	FRUIT	GRAIN	MEAT/ FISH	NUT/SEED/ BEAN	WATER	SWEET	FRIED

SATURDAY ____ / ____ / ____

RESTING HEART RATE _____ WEIGHT _____

DISTANCE _____   TIME _____   PACE/SPLITS _____   INTENSITY FACTOR _____

Notes _____

_____

_____

_____

_____

_____

ACHES AND PAINS _____

Rating	GREAT	VERY GOOD	GOOD	FAIR	POOR	VERY BAD

Nutrition	VEGGIE	FRUIT	GRAIN	MEAT/ FISH	NUT/SEED/ BEAN	WATER	SWEET	FRIED

SUNDAY _____ / _____ / _____

RESTING HEART RATE _____   WEIGHT _____

DISTANCE _____   TIME _____   PACE/SPLITS _____   INTENSITY FACTOR _____

Notes _____

_____

_____

_____

_____

ACHES AND PAINS _____

Rating	GREAT	VERY GOOD		GOOD	FAIR	POOR	VERY BAD

Nutrition	VEGGIE	FRUIT	GRAIN	MEAT/FISH	NUT/SEED/BEAN	WATER	SWEET	FRIED

WEEKLY SUMMARY

AVERAGE INTENSITY FACTOR _____

	WEEKLY TOTAL	YEAR TO DATE
RUN DISTANCE		
RUN TIME		
OTHER TRAINING		
TOTAL TIME		

Notes _____

_____

_____

_____

_____

MONDAY	TUESDAY	WEDNESDAY	THURSDAY

FRIDAY	SATURDAY	SUNDAY	
			TOTAL DISTANCE
			TOTAL DISTANCE
			TOTAL DISTANCE
			TOTAL DISTANCE

MONDAY ___ / ___ / ___   RESTING HEART RATE _____ WEIGHT _____

DISTANCE _____   TIME _____   PACE/SPLITS _____   INTENSITY FACTOR _____

Notes _____

_____

_____

_____

ACHES AND PAINS _____

Rating	GREAT	VERY GOOD	GOOD	FAIR	POOR	VERY BAD

Nutrition	VEGGIE	FRUIT	GRAIN	MEAT/ FISH	NUT/SEED/ BEAN	WATER	SWEET	FRIED

TUESDAY ___ / ___ / ___   RESTING HEART RATE _____ WEIGHT _____

DISTANCE _____   TIME _____   PACE/SPLITS _____   INTENSITY FACTOR _____

Notes _____

_____

_____

_____

ACHES AND PAINS _____

Rating	GREAT	VERY GOOD	GOOD	FAIR	POOR	VERY BAD

Nutrition	VEGGIE	FRUIT	GRAIN	MEAT/ FISH	NUT/SEED/ BEAN	WATER	SWEET	FRIED

ultramarathon as part of your training for a marathon. Just be sure to take it slow so you don't trash your legs and spoil your training for the next week.

WEDNESDAY ___/___/___   RESTING HEART RATE _____ WEIGHT _____

DISTANCE _____   TIME _____   PACE/SPLITS _____   INTENSITY FACTOR _____

Notes _____

_____

_____

_____

ACHES AND PAINS _____

Rating	GREAT	VERY GOOD	GOOD	FAIR	POOR	VERY BAD

Nutrition	VEGGIE	FRUIT	GRAIN	MEAT/ FISH	NUT/SEED/ BEAN	WATER	SWEET	FRIED

THURSDAY ___/___/___   RESTING HEART RATE _____ WEIGHT _____

DISTANCE _____   TIME _____   PACE/SPLITS _____   INTENSITY FACTOR _____

Notes _____

_____

_____

_____

ACHES AND PAINS _____

Rating	GREAT	VERY GOOD	GOOD	FAIR	POOR	VERY BAD

Nutrition	VEGGIE	FRUIT	GRAIN	MEAT/ FISH	NUT/SEED/ BEAN	WATER	SWEET	FRIED

FRIDAY ___ / ___ / ___

RESTING HEART RATE _____ WEIGHT _____

DISTANCE _____ TIME _____ PACE/SPLITS _____ INTENSITY FACTOR _____

Notes _____

_____

_____

_____

_____

ACHES AND PAINS _____

Rating	GREAT	VERY GOOD	GOOD	FAIR	POOR	VERY BAD

Nutrition	VEGGIE	FRUIT	GRAIN	MEAT/FISH	NUT/SEED/BEAN	WATER	SWEET	FRIED

SATURDAY ___ / ___ / ___

RESTING HEART RATE _____ WEIGHT _____

DISTANCE _____ TIME _____ PACE/SPLITS _____ INTENSITY FACTOR _____

Notes _____

_____

_____

_____

_____

ACHES AND PAINS _____

Rating	GREAT	VERY GOOD	GOOD	FAIR	POOR	VERY BAD

Nutrition	VEGGIE	FRUIT	GRAIN	MEAT/FISH	NUT/SEED/BEAN	WATER	SWEET	FRIED

SUNDAY ___ / ___ / ___

RESTING HEART RATE _____ WEIGHT _____

DISTANCE _____ TIME _____ PACE/SPLITS _____ INTENSITY FACTOR _____

Notes _____

_____

_____

_____

_____

_____

ACHES AND PAINS _____

Rating	GREAT	VERY GOOD		GOOD	FAIR		POOR	VERY BAD
Nutrition	VEGGIE	FRUIT	GRAIN	MEAT/FISH	NUT/SEED/BEAN	WATER	SWEET	FRIED

WEEKLY SUMMARY

AVERAGE INTENSITY FACTOR _____

	WEEKLY TOTAL	YEAR TO DATE
RUN DISTANCE		
RUN TIME		
OTHER TRAINING		
TOTAL TIME		

Notes _____

_____

_____

_____

_____

_____

MONDAY ___ / ___ / ___   RESTING HEART RATE _____ WEIGHT _____

DISTANCE _____   TIME _____   PACE/SPLITS _____   INTENSITY FACTOR _____

Notes _____

_____

_____

_____

ACHES AND PAINS _____

Rating	GREAT	VERY GOOD		GOOD	FAIR	POOR	VERY BAD
Nutrition	VEGGIE	FRUIT	GRAIN	MEAT/ FISH	NUT/SEED/ BEAN	WATER	SWEET	FRIED

TUESDAY ___ / ___ / ___   RESTING HEART RATE _____ WEIGHT _____

DISTANCE _____   TIME _____   PACE/SPLITS _____   INTENSITY FACTOR _____

Notes _____

_____

_____

_____

ACHES AND PAINS _____

Rating	GREAT	VERY GOOD		GOOD	FAIR	POOR	VERY BAD
Nutrition	VEGGIE	FRUIT	GRAIN	MEAT/ FISH	NUT/SEED/ BEAN	WATER	SWEET	FRIED

too much strain from concentrating in particular areas of your legs. There's no scientific proof that shoe rotation works, but there's also no proof that it doesn't work, and it can't hurt to try it for yourself.

WEDNESDAY ____ / ____ / ____   RESTING HEART RATE _____ WEIGHT _____

DISTANCE _____   TIME _____   PACE/SPLITS _____   INTENSITY FACTOR _____

Notes _____

_____

_____

_____

ACHES AND PAINS _____

Rating	GREAT	VERY GOOD	GOOD	FAIR	POOR	VERY BAD

Nutrition	VEGGIE	FRUIT	GRAIN	MEAT/FISH	NUT/SEED/BEAN	WATER	SWEET	FRIED

THURSDAY ____ / ____ / ____   RESTING HEART RATE _____ WEIGHT _____

DISTANCE _____   TIME _____   PACE/SPLITS _____   INTENSITY FACTOR _____

Notes _____

_____

_____

_____

ACHES AND PAINS _____

Rating	GREAT	VERY GOOD	GOOD	FAIR	POOR	VERY BAD

Nutrition	VEGGIE	FRUIT	GRAIN	MEAT/FISH	NUT/SEED/BEAN	WATER	SWEET	FRIED

FRIDAY ___ / ___ / ___

RESTING HEART RATE _____ WEIGHT _____

DISTANCE _____ TIME _____ PACE/SPLITS _____ INTENSITY FACTOR _____

Notes _____

_____

_____

_____

_____

ACHES AND PAINS _____

Rating	GREAT	VERY GOOD		GOOD	FAIR	POOR		VERY BAD
Nutrition	VEGGIE	FRUIT	GRAIN	MEAT/ FISH	NUT/SEED/ BEAN	WATER	SWEET	FRIED

SATURDAY ___ / ___ / ___

RESTING HEART RATE _____ WEIGHT _____

DISTANCE _____ TIME _____ PACE/SPLITS _____ INTENSITY FACTOR _____

Notes _____

_____

_____

_____

_____

ACHES AND PAINS _____

Rating	GREAT	VERY GOOD		GOOD	FAIR	POOR		VERY BAD
Nutrition	VEGGIE	FRUIT	GRAIN	MEAT/ FISH	NUT/SEED/ BEAN	WATER	SWEET	FRIED

SUNDAY ___ / ___ / ___

RESTING HEART RATE _____ WEIGHT _____

DISTANCE _____   TIME _____   PACE/SPLITS _____   INTENSITY FACTOR _____

Notes _____

_____

_____

_____

_____

ACHES AND PAINS _____

Rating	GREAT	VERY GOOD		GOOD	FAIR		POOR	VERY BAD
Nutrition	VEGGIE	FRUIT	GRAIN	MEAT/FISH	NUT/SEED/BEAN	WATER	SWEET	FRIED

WEEKLY SUMMARY

AVERAGE INTENSITY FACTOR _____

	WEEKLY TOTAL	YEAR TO DATE
RUN DISTANCE		
RUN TIME		
OTHER TRAINING		
TOTAL TIME		

Notes _____

_____

_____

_____

_____

MONDAY ___ / ___ / ___   RESTING HEART RATE _____ WEIGHT _____

DISTANCE _____   TIME _____   PACE/SPLITS _____   INTENSITY FACTOR _____

Notes _____

_____

_____

_____

ACHES AND PAINS _____

Rating	GREAT	VERY GOOD		GOOD	FAIR		POOR		VERY BAD
Nutrition	VEGGIE	FRUIT	GRAIN	MEAT/ FISH	NUT/SEED/ BEAN	WATER	SWEET	FRIED	

TUESDAY ___ / ___ / ___   RESTING HEART RATE _____ WEIGHT _____

DISTANCE _____   TIME _____   PACE/SPLITS _____   INTENSITY FACTOR _____

Notes _____

_____

_____

_____

ACHES AND PAINS _____

Rating	GREAT	VERY GOOD		GOOD	FAIR		POOR		VERY BAD
Nutrition	VEGGIE	FRUIT	GRAIN	MEAT/ FISH	NUT/SEED/ BEAN	WATER	SWEET	FRIED	

254

running, so the damage builds and builds until a breakdown occurs. To avoid this problem, aim to get 25 to 30 percent of your daily calories from fat.

WEDNESDAY ____/____/____   RESTING HEART RATE _____ WEIGHT _____

DISTANCE _____   TIME _____   PACE/SPLITS _____   INTENSITY FACTOR _____

Notes _____

_____

_____

_____

ACHES AND PAINS _____

Rating	GREAT	VERY GOOD		GOOD	FAIR		POOR		VERY BAD
Nutrition	VEGGIE	FRUIT	GRAIN	MEAT/FISH	NUT/SEED/BEAN	WATER	SWEET	FRIED

THURSDAY ____/____/____   RESTING HEART RATE _____ WEIGHT _____

DISTANCE _____   TIME _____   PACE/SPLITS _____   INTENSITY FACTOR _____

Notes _____

_____

_____

_____

ACHES AND PAINS _____

Rating	GREAT	VERY GOOD		GOOD	FAIR		POOR		VERY BAD
Nutrition	VEGGIE	FRUIT	GRAIN	MEAT/FISH	NUT/SEED/BEAN	WATER	SWEET	FRIED

FRIDAY ___ / ___ / ___

RESTING HEART RATE _____ WEIGHT _____

DISTANCE _____ TIME _____ PACE/SPLITS _____ INTENSITY FACTOR _____

Notes _____

_____

_____

_____

_____

ACHES AND PAINS _____

Rating	GREAT	VERY GOOD	GOOD	FAIR	POOR	VERY BAD

Nutrition	VEGGIE	FRUIT	GRAIN	MEAT/FISH	NUT/SEED/BEAN	WATER	SWEET	FRIED

SATURDAY ___ / ___ / ___

RESTING HEART RATE _____ WEIGHT _____

DISTANCE _____ TIME _____ PACE/SPLITS _____ INTENSITY FACTOR _____

Notes _____

_____

_____

_____

_____

ACHES AND PAINS _____

Rating	GREAT	VERY GOOD	GOOD	FAIR	POOR	VERY BAD

Nutrition	VEGGIE	FRUIT	GRAIN	MEAT/FISH	NUT/SEED/BEAN	WATER	SWEET	FRIED

SUNDAY ___ / ___ / ___

RESTING HEART RATE _____ WEIGHT _____

DISTANCE _____ TIME _____ PACE/SPLITS _____ INTENSITY FACTOR _____

Notes _____

_____

_____

_____

_____

_____

ACHES AND PAINS _____

Rating	GREAT	VERY GOOD		GOOD	FAIR		POOR	VERY BAD
Nutrition	VEGGIE	FRUIT	GRAIN	MEAT/ FISH	NUT/SEED/ BEAN	WATER	SWEET	FRIED

WEEKLY SUMMARY

AVERAGE INTENSITY FACTOR _____

	WEEKLY TOTAL	YEAR TO DATE
RUN DISTANCE		
RUN TIME		
OTHER TRAINING		
TOTAL TIME		

Notes _____

_____

_____

_____

_____

MONDAY ___ / ___ / ___

RESTING HEART RATE _____ WEIGHT _____

DISTANCE _____ TIME _____ PACE/SPLITS _____ INTENSITY FACTOR _____

Notes _____

_____

_____

_____

ACHES AND PAINS _____

Rating GREAT VERY GOOD GOOD FAIR POOR VERY BAD

Nutrition	VEGGIE	FRUIT	GRAIN	MEAT/FISH	NUT/SEED/BEAN	WATER	SWEET	FRIED

TUESDAY ___ / ___ / ___

RESTING HEART RATE _____ WEIGHT _____

DISTANCE _____ TIME _____ PACE/SPLITS _____ INTENSITY FACTOR _____

Notes _____

_____

_____

_____

ACHES AND PAINS _____

Rating GREAT VERY GOOD GOOD FAIR POOR VERY BAD

Nutrition	VEGGIE	FRUIT	GRAIN	MEAT/FISH	NUT/SEED/BEAN	WATER	SWEET	FRIED

the day before a race to slightly deplete your muscle glycogen stores and stimulate a carbohydrate sponging effect. Consume a bunch of carbs immediately afterward and at each subsequent meal until your race.

WEDNESDAY _____ / _____ / _____   RESTING HEART RATE _____   WEIGHT _____

DISTANCE _____   TIME _____   PACE/SPLITS _____   INTENSITY FACTOR _____

Notes _____

_____

_____

_____

ACHES AND PAINS _____

Rating	GREAT	VERY GOOD		GOOD	FAIR	POOR	VERY BAD
Nutrition	VEGGIE	FRUIT	GRAIN	MEAT/ FISH	NUT/SEED/ BEAN	WATER	SWEET	FRIED

THURSDAY _____ / _____ / _____   RESTING HEART RATE _____   WEIGHT _____

DISTANCE _____   TIME _____   PACE/SPLITS _____   INTENSITY FACTOR _____

Notes _____

_____

_____

_____

ACHES AND PAINS _____

Rating	GREAT	VERY GOOD		GOOD	FAIR	POOR	VERY BAD
Nutrition	VEGGIE	FRUIT	GRAIN	MEAT/ FISH	NUT/SEED/ BEAN	WATER	SWEET	FRIED

FRIDAY ___/___/___

RESTING HEART RATE _____ WEIGHT _____

DISTANCE _____ TIME _____ PACE/SPLITS _____ INTENSITY FACTOR _____

Notes _____

_____

_____

_____

_____

ACHES AND PAINS _____

Rating	GREAT		VERY GOOD		GOOD		FAIR		POOR		VERY BAD
Nutrition	VEGGIE	FRUIT	GRAIN	MEAT/ FISH	NUT/SEED/ BEAN	WATER	SWEET	FRIED

SATURDAY ___/___/___

RESTING HEART RATE _____ WEIGHT _____

DISTANCE _____ TIME _____ PACE/SPLITS _____ INTENSITY FACTOR _____

Notes _____

_____

_____

_____

_____

ACHES AND PAINS _____

Rating	GREAT		VERY GOOD		GOOD		FAIR		POOR		VERY BAD
Nutrition	VEGGIE	FRUIT	GRAIN	MEAT/ FISH	NUT/SEED/ BEAN	WATER	SWEET	FRIED

SUNDAY ___ / ___ / ___

RESTING HEART RATE _____ WEIGHT _____

DISTANCE _____ TIME _____ PACE/SPLITS _____ INTENSITY FACTOR _____

Notes _____

_____

_____

_____

_____

ACHES AND PAINS _____

Rating

| GREAT | VERY GOOD | GOOD | FAIR | POOR | VERY BAD |

Nutrition

| VEGGIE | FRUIT | GRAIN | MEAT/ FISH | NUT/SEED/ BEAN | WATER | SWEET | FRIED |

WEEKLY SUMMARY

AVERAGE INTENSITY FACTOR _____

	WEEKLY TOTAL	YEAR TO DATE
RUN DISTANCE		
RUN TIME		
OTHER TRAINING		
TOTAL TIME		

Notes _____

_____

_____

_____

_____

261

MONDAY ___ / ___ / ___

RESTING HEART RATE _____ WEIGHT _____

DISTANCE _____ TIME _____ PACE/SPLITS _____ INTENSITY FACTOR _____

Notes _____

_____

_____

_____

ACHES AND PAINS _____

Rating GREAT VERY GOOD GOOD FAIR POOR VERY BAD

Nutrition | VEGGIE | FRUIT | GRAIN | MEAT/FISH | NUT/SEED/BEAN | WATER | SWEET | FRIED |

TUESDAY ___ / ___ / ___

RESTING HEART RATE _____ WEIGHT _____

DISTANCE _____ TIME _____ PACE/SPLITS _____ INTENSITY FACTOR _____

Notes _____

_____

_____

_____

ACHES AND PAINS _____

Rating GREAT VERY GOOD GOOD FAIR POOR VERY BAD

Nutrition | VEGGIE | FRUIT | GRAIN | MEAT/FISH | NUT/SEED/BEAN | WATER | SWEET | FRIED |

so on. Most colds and flus are caught through "self-contamination," not by breathing germ-filled air.

WEDNESDAY ___ / ___ / ___   RESTING HEART RATE _____ WEIGHT _____

DISTANCE _____   TIME _____   PACE/SPLITS _____   INTENSITY FACTOR _____

Notes _____

_____

_____

_____

ACHES AND PAINS _____

Rating	GREAT	VERY GOOD		GOOD	FAIR	POOR	VERY BAD

Nutrition	VEGGIE	FRUIT	GRAIN	MEAT/ FISH	NUT/SEED/ BEAN	WATER	SWEET	FRIED

THURSDAY ___ / ___ / ___   RESTING HEART RATE _____ WEIGHT _____

DISTANCE _____   TIME _____   PACE/SPLITS _____   INTENSITY FACTOR _____

Notes _____

_____

_____

_____

ACHES AND PAINS _____

Rating	GREAT	VERY GOOD		GOOD	FAIR	POOR	VERY BAD

Nutrition	VEGGIE	FRUIT	GRAIN	MEAT/ FISH	NUT/SEED/ BEAN	WATER	SWEET	FRIED

FRIDAY ___ / ___ / ___   RESTING HEART RATE _____ WEIGHT _____

DISTANCE _____   TIME _____   PACE/SPLITS _____   INTENSITY FACTOR _____

Notes _____

_____

_____

_____

_____

ACHES AND PAINS _____

Rating	GREAT	VERY GOOD	GOOD	FAIR	POOR	VERY BAD

Nutrition	VEGGIE	FRUIT	GRAIN	MEAT/ FISH	NUT/SEED/ BEAN	WATER	SWEET	FRIED

SATURDAY ___ / ___ / ___   RESTING HEART RATE _____ WEIGHT _____

DISTANCE _____   TIME _____   PACE/SPLITS _____   INTENSITY FACTOR _____

Notes _____

_____

_____

_____

_____

ACHES AND PAINS _____

Rating	GREAT	VERY GOOD	GOOD	FAIR	POOR	VERY BAD

Nutrition	VEGGIE	FRUIT	GRAIN	MEAT/ FISH	NUT/SEED/ BEAN	WATER	SWEET	FRIED

SUNDAY ____ / ____ / ____

RESTING HEART RATE _____ WEIGHT _____

DISTANCE _____ TIME _____ PACE/SPLITS _____ INTENSITY FACTOR _____

Notes _____

ACHES AND PAINS _____

Rating	GREAT	VERY GOOD	GOOD	FAIR	POOR	VERY BAD

Nutrition	VEGGIE	FRUIT	GRAIN	MEAT/FISH	NUT/SEED/BEAN	WATER	SWEET	FRIED

WEEKLY SUMMARY

AVERAGE INTENSITY FACTOR _____

	WEEKLY TOTAL	YEAR TO DATE
RUN DISTANCE		
RUN TIME		
OTHER TRAINING		
TOTAL TIME		

Notes _____

265

[A] Running Workouts

There are 11 basic types of runs that you will want to use in your training program: recovery runs, base runs, long runs, progression runs, marathon-pace runs, fartlek runs, hill repetitions, threshold runs, specific endurance intervals, speed intervals, and mixed intervals. Following are brief descriptions of each. See Appendix B for more information about recommended pace levels.

Recovery run. A recovery run is a relatively short run performed at a steady, comfortable pace. Recovery runs are best done the day after a hard key workout. Example: 4 miles at recovery pace.

Base run. A base run is a relatively short to moderate-length run undertaken at a steady, moderate pace. Base runs are your bread-and-butter aerobic fitness builders. Example: 6 miles at base pace.

Long run. A long run is simply a base run that lasts long enough to leave you moderately to severely fatigued. Long runs develop raw endurance. Example: 15 miles at base pace.

Progression run. A progression run is a run that begins at a moderate pace and ends with a short segment of faster running. Progression runs provide a moderate training stimulus when your body is ready for more than an easy run but is not ready for a hard key workout. Example: 5 miles at base pace + 1 mile at half-marathon pace.

Marathon-pace run. A marathon-pace run is just that: a prolonged run at marathon pace. It's a good workout to perform at a very challenging level in the final weeks of preparation for a marathon. Example: 1 mile at base pace + 8 miles at marathon pace.

Fartlek run. A fartlek run is a base run sprinkled with short, fast intervals—usually 30 to 60 seconds at 10K to 1500m pace. Fartlek runs provide the same benefits as interval runs (increased speed, improved fatigue resistance at faster speeds) but are generally easier because they include less high-intensity running.

Hill repetitions. Hill repetitions are essentially intervals run uphill. They provide the same benefits as interval runs but they also build more strength. Example: 1-mile warm-up at recovery pace + 6 x 400m uphill at 1500m effort (i.e. same effort as in a 1500m race, but a slower pace due to the hill) with 400m active recoveries at recovery pace + 1-mile cool-down at recovery pace.

Similar to hill repetitions are short hill sprints, consisting of 10-second all-out sprints up a steep hill. These are great power developers, but they are too intense to make a complete workout of them. I recommend that you do one set of steep hill sprints per week immediately after completing a recovery or base run.

Threshold run. A threshold run is a workout that features one or two sustained efforts at half-marathon to 10K pace. Threshold runs serve to increase the pace you can sustain for a prolonged period of time and to increase the time you can sustain a relatively fast pace. Example: 1-mile warm-up at recovery pace + 3.5 miles @ 10K pace + 1-mile cool-down at recovery pace.

Specific endurance intervals. Specific endurance intervals take the form of relatively short to moderately long intervals (200 meters to 1 km) at 5K or 10K pace. They're an excellent means of progressively developing efficiency and fatigue resistance at fast running speeds.

Speed intervals. Speed intervals are short or relatively short intervals (100 to 400m) run at 1500m pace. Example: 1-mile warm-up at recovery pace + 12 x 400m at 1500m pace with 400m active recoveries at recovery pace + 1-mile cool-down at recovery pace.

Mixed intervals. Mixed intervals, as the name suggests, are intervals of various distances run at different pace levels between half-marathon pace and 1500m pace. Mixed interval runs are an excellent means of including a variety of training stimuli within a single workout. Example: 1-mile warm-up at recovery pace + 400m at 1500m pace/800m at 3000m pace/1K at 5K pace/1 mile at 10K pace with 400m active recoveries at recovery pace + 1-mile cool-down at recovery pace.

B | Target Pace Level

It's important that your training program incorporate a balance of running at different speeds. Each workout you do should have one or more specific pace targets, as hitting these targets will ensure that you get the desired training effect from the workout. The target pace level (TPL) system is a simple tool that you can use for this purpose. I created it by slightly modifying the groundbreaking work of the great running coach Jack Daniels, PhD, whose original "VDOT" pacing system is still one of the best. The big difference between VDOT and TPL is that the former uses physiology-based pace targets (e.g., "lactate threshold pace"), whereas TPL uses performance-based targets (e.g., 10K pace).

In the TPL system, a unique number between 50 and 1 is assigned to each running performance level from back of the pack (TPL 50) to world class (TPL 1). The first step in using this system is to go to Table 1 and find your current TPL level by looking up a recent race time at the 5K, 10K, half-marathon, or marathon distance that equates to your *current* fitness level, or by estimating your finishing time at one of these distances given your *current* fitness level.

Once you have determined your current TPL number, go to Table 2 to find the workout TPLs associated with it (Table 2a is pace per mile and Table 2b is pace per kilometer). Let's say you ran a 10K as a tune-up race in your previous training cycle, when your fitness level was roughly where it is now, and your finishing time was 47:11. This time falls between TPL 38 and TPL 37 on the table. Since it's closer to TPL 37, it is probably most sensible to use the TPL 37 workout target pace levels initially in your next training cycle.

Use recovery pace in your recovery workouts. Use base pace in base runs and in most endurance runs. Use marathon pace in marathon-pace endurance runs and progression runs. Use half-marathon pace and 10K pace in threshold runs, progression runs, and longer interval runs. Use 5K pace, 3K pace, and 1500m pace in shorter interval runs, hill repetition runs, and fartlek runs.

You will need to adjust your TPL number as you build fitness over the course of a training cycle. As your running fitness goes up, your TPL number will go down and your

TPLs will become faster. There are two ways you can go about making these adjustments. The formal way is to run a race or time trial once every four weeks or so and use the result to adjust your TPL. A less formal and no less effective way is to let your workout performances—and especially your key workout performances—guide you. When your target paces become consistently too easy, you know it's time to lower your TPL score.

TABLE 1 Determine Your Target Pace Level

TPL	5K Time	10K Time	Half-Marathon Time	Marathon Time
50	30:40	1:03:46	2:21:04	4:49:17
49	29:51	1:02:03	2:17:21	4:41:57
48	29:05	1:00:26	2:13:49	4:34:59
47	28:21	58:54	2:10:27	4:28:22
46	27:39	57:26	2:07:16	4:22:03
45	27:00	56:03	2:04:13	4:16:03
44	26:22	54:44	2:01:19	4:10:19
43	25:46	53:29	1:58:34	4:04:50
42	25:12	52:17	1:55:55	3:59:35
41	24:39	51:09	1:53:24	3:54:34
40	24:08	50:03	1:50:59	3:49:45
39	23:38	49:01	1:48:40	3:45:09
38	23:09	48:01	1:46:27	3:40:43
37	22:41	47:04	1:44:20	3:36:28
36	22:15	46:09	1:42:17	3:32:23
35	21:50	45:16	1:40:20	3:28:26
34	21:25	44:25	1:38:27	3:24:39
33	21:02	43:36	1:36:38	3:21:00
32	20:39	42:50	1:34:53	3:17:29
31	20:18	42:04	1:33:12	3:14:06
30	19:57	41:21	1:31:35	3:10:49
29	19:36	40:39	1:30:02	3:07:39

CONTINUES

TABLE 1 Determine Your Target Pace Level

TPL	5K Time	10K Time	Half-Marathon Time	Marathon Time
28	19:17	39:59	1:28:31	3:04:36
27	18:58	39:20	1:27:04	3:01:39
26	18:40	38:42	1:25:40	2:58:47
25	18:22	38:06	1:24:18	2:56:01
24	18:05	37:31	1:23:00	2:53:20
23	17:49	36:57	1:21:43	2:50:45
22	17:33	36:24	1:20:30	2:48:14
21	17:17	35:52	1:19:18	2:45:47
20	17:03	35:22	1:18:09	2:43:25
19	16:48	34:52	1:17:02	2:41:08
18	16:34	34:23	1:15:57	2:38:54
17	16:20	33:55	1:14:54	2:36:44
16	16:07	33:28	1:13:53	2:34:38
15	15:54	33:01	1:12:53	2:32:35
14	15:42	32:35	1:11:56	2:30:36
13	15:29	32:11	1:11:00	2:28:40
12	15:18	31:46	1:10:05	2:26:47
11	15:06	31:23	1:09:12	2:24:57
10	14:55	31:00	1:08:21	2:23:10
9	14:44	30:38	1:07:31	2:21:26
8	14:33	30:16	1:06:42	2:19:44
7	14:23	29:55	1:05:54	2:18:05
6	14:13	29:34	1:05:08	2:16:29
5	14:03	29:14	1:04:23	2:14:55
4	13:54	28:55	1:03:39	2:13:23
3	13:44	28:36	1:02:56	2:11:54
2	13:35	28:17	1:02:15	2:10:27
1	13:26	27:59	1:01:34	2:09:02

TABLE 2a Find Your Target Pace Zones (pace per mile)

TPL	Recovery	Base Pace	26.2-Mile Pace	13.1-Mile Pace	10K Pace	5K Pace	3K Pace	1500-Meter Pace
50	14:03–12:43	12:42–11:39	11:02	10:45	10:15	9:52 (2:27)	9:37 (2:23)	9:11 (2:17)
49	13:45–12:25	12:24–11:22	10:45	10:28	9:59	9:36 (2:23)	9:21 (2:19)	8:55 (2:13)
48	13:27–12:07	12:06–11:05	10:29	10:12	9:43	9:21 (2:19)	9:06 (2:15)	8:41 (2:10)
47	13:11–11:51	11:50–10:50	10:14	9:57	9:28	9:07 (2:15)	8:52 (2:12)	8:27 (2:06)
46	12:50–11:30	11:29–10:34	10:00	9:42	9:14	8:53 (2:12)	8:39 (2:09)	8:14 (2:03)
45	12:41–11:21	11:20–10:21	9:45	9:28	9:01	8:41 (2:09)	8:26 (2:06)	8:01 (2:00)
44	12:25–11:05	11:04–10:07	9:33	9:15	8:48	8:29 (2:06)	8:15 (2:03)	7:49 (1:57)
43	12:12–10:52	10:51–9:54	9:20	9:02	8:36	8:17 (2:03)	8:03 (2:00)	7:38 (1:54)
42	11:59–10:39	10:38–9:41	9:08	8:50	8:24	8:06 (2:00)	7:52 (1:57)	7:27 (1:51)
41	11:47–10:27	10:26–9:30	8:56	8:39	8:13	7:56 (1:58)	7:41 (1:54)	7:17 (1:49)
40	11:30–10:15	10:14–9:18	8:46	8:27	8:03	7:46 (1:55)	7:32 (1:52)	7:07 (1:46)
39	11:19–10:04	10:03–9:08	8:35	8:17	7:53	7:36 (1:53)	7:22 (1:50)	6:58 (1:44)
38	11:07–9:52	9:51–8:57	8:25	8:07	7:43	7:27 (1:51)	7:13 (1:47)	6:49 (1:42)
37	10:57–9:42	9:43–8:47	8:15	7:57	7:34	7:18 (1:48)	7:04 (1:45)	6:41 (1:40)
36	10:46–9:31	9:30–8:37	8:06	7:48	7:25	7:09 (1:46)	6:55 (1:43)	6:32 (1:38)
35	10:37–9:22	9:21–8:28	7:57	7:39	7:17	7:01 (1:44)	6:47 (1:41)	6:25 (1:36)
34	10:27–9:12	9:11–8:18	7:48	7:30	7:08	6:53 (1:42)	6:40 (1:39)	6:17 (1:34)
33	10:17–9:02	9:01–8:10	7:40	7:22	7:01	6:46 (1:40)	6:32 (1:37)	6:10 (1:32)
32	10:08–8:53	8:52–8:02	7:32	7:14	6:53	6:38 (1:38)	6:25 (1:35)	6:03 (1:30)
31	10:00–8:45	8:46–7:53	7:24	7:06	6:46	6:32 (1:37)	6:18 (1:34)	5:56 (1:29)

TABLE 2a Find Your Target Pace Zones (pace per mile)

TPL	Recovery	Base Pace	26.2-Mile Pace	13.1-Mile Pace	10K Pace	5K Pace	3K Pace	1500-Meter Pace
30	9:47–8:37	8:36–7:46	7:17	6:59	6:39	6:25 (1:35)	6:11 (1:32)	5:50 (1:27)
29	9:40–8:30	8:29–7:38	7:09	6:52	6:32	6:18 (1:33)	6:05 (1:30)	5:44 (1:26)
28	9:31–8:21	8:20–7:31	7:02	6:45	6:26	6:12 (1:32)	5:58 (1:29)	5:38 (1:24)
27	9:24–8:14	8:13–7:24	6:56	6:38	6:19	6:06 (1:31)	5:52 (1:27)	5:32 (1:23)
26	9:17–8:07	8:06–7:17	6:49	6:32	6:13	6:00 (1:30)	5:47 (1:26)	5:27 (1:21)
25	9:10–8:00	7:59–7:11	6:43	6:25	6:07	5:54 (1:28)	5:41 (1:24)	5:21 (1:20)
24	9:03–7:53	7:52–7:04	6:37	6:19	6:02	5:49 (1:26)	5:36 (1:23)	5:16 (1:19)
23	8:56–7:46	7:45–6:58	6:31	6:14	5:56	5:44 (1:25)	5:31 (1:22)	5:11 (1:17)
22	8:50–7:40	7:39–6:52	6:25	6:08	5:51	5:38 (1:24)	5:26 (1:21)	5:06 (1:16)
21	8:44–7:34	7:33–6:44	6:19	6:02	5:46	5:33 (1:22)	5:20 (1:19)	5:02 (1:15)
20	8:33–7:28	7:27–6:39	6:14	5:57	5:41	5:29 (1:21)	5:16 (1:18)	4:57 (1:14)
19	8:26–7:21	7:20–6:35	6:09	5:52	5:36	5:24 (1:20)	5:11 (1:17)	4:53 (1:13)
18	8:21–7:16	7:15–6:30	6:04	5:47	5:32	5:19 (1:19)	5:07 (1:16)	4:49 (1:12)
17	8:15–7:10	7:09–6:25	5:59	5:42	5:27	5:15 (1:18)	5:03 (1:15)	4:45 (1:11)
16	8:10–7:05	7:04–6:20	5:54	5:38	5:23	5:11 (1:17)	4:58 (1:14)	4:41 (1:10)
15	8:04–6:59	6:58–6:15	5:49	5:33	5:18	5:07 (1:16)	4:54 (1:13)	4:37 (1:09)
14	7:59–6:54	6:53–6:10	5:45	5:29	5:14	5:03 (1:15)	4:50 (1:12)	4:33 (1:08)
13	7:53–6:48	6:47–6:05	5:40	5:24	5:10	4:59 (1:14)	4:47 (1:11)	4:30 (1:07)
12	7:49–6:44	6:43–6:01	5:36	5:20	5:06	4:55 (1:13)	4:43 (1:10)	4:26 (1:06)
11	7:44–6:39	6:38–5:57	5:32	5:16	5:03	4:51 (1:12)	4:39 (1:09)	4:23 (1:05)

CONTINUES

TPL	Recovery	Base Pace	26.2-Mile Pace	13.1-Mile Pace	10K Pace	5K Pace	3K Pace	1500-Meter Pace
10	7:35–6:35	6:34–5:53	5:28	5:12	4:59	4:48 (1:12)	4:35 (1:08)	4:19 (1:04)
9	7:29–6:29	6:28–5:48	5:24	5:09	4:55	4:44 (1:10)	4:32 (1:07)	4:16 (1:04)
8	7:25–6:25	6:24–6:44	5:20	5:05	4:52	4:40 (1:09)	4:29 (1:06)	4:13 (1:03)
7	7:21–6:21	6:20–5:40	5:16	5:01	4:48	4:37 (1:09)	4:26 (1:06)	4:10 (1:02)
6	7:16–6:16	6:15–5:36	5:12	4:58	4:45	4:34 (1:08)	4:22 (1:05)	4:07 (1:01)
5	7:12–6:12	6:11–5:33	5:09	4:54	4:42	4:31 (1:07)	4:19 (1:04)	4:04 (1:01)
4	7:08–6:08	6:07–5:29	5:05	4:51	4:39	4:28 (1:06)	4:16 (1:03)	4:02 (1:00)
3	7:03–6:03	6:02–5:25	5:01	4:48	4:36	4:25 (1:05)	4:13 (1:03)	3:58 (0:59)
2	7:00–6:00	5:59–5:22	4:58	4:44	4:33	4:22 (1:05)	4:11 (1:02)	3:56 (0:59)
1	6:57–5:57	5:56–5:19	4:55	4:41	4:30	4:19 (1:04)	4:08 (1:01)	3:53 (0:58)

Note: Numbers in parentheses are pace per 400m. For ease of use, the 400m time is calculated for 5K, 3K, and 1500m paces because intervals run at these faster paces are typically shorter in length. For example, a TPL 35 runner doing six 800m intervals at his or her 5K pace would be attempting to run each 800 as close to 3:28 as possible.

TABLE 2b Find Your Target Pace Zones (pace per kilometer)

TPL	Recovery	Base Pace	26.2-Mile Pace	13.1-Mile Pace	10K Pace	5K Pace	3K Pace	1500-Meter Pace
50	8:44–7:54	7:53–7:14	6:52	6:41	6:22	6:08 (2:27)*	5:59 (2:23)	5:42 (2:17)
49	8:32–7:43	7:42–7:03	6:41	6:30	6:12	5:58 (2:23)	5:48 (2:19)	5:32 (2:13)
48	8:21–7:32	7:31–6:53	6:31	6:20	6:02	5:48 (2:19)	5:39 (2:15)	5:24 (2:10)
47	8:11–7:21	7:21–6:44	6:21	6:11	5:53	5:39 (2:15)	5:30 (2:12)	5:15 (2:06)
46	7:58–7:09	7:08–6:34	6:12	6:02	5:44	5:31 (2:12)	5:22 (2:09)	5:07 (2:03)
45	7:53–7:03	7:02–6:26	6:04	5:53	5:36	5:24 (2:09)	5:14 (2:06)	4:59 (2:00)
44	7:43–6:53	6:53–6:17	5:56	5:45	5:28	5:16 (2:06)	5:08 (2:03)	4:51 (1:57)
43	7:35–6:45	6:44–6:09	5:48	5:36	5:20	5:09 (2:03)	5:00 (2:00)	4:44 (1:54)
42	7:27–6:37	6:36–6:01	5:35	5:29	5:13	5:02 (2:00)	4:53 (1:57)	4:38 (1:51)
41	7:19–6:29	6:29–5:54	5:33	5:22	5:06	4:56 (1:58)	4:46 (1:54)	4:32 (1:49)
40	7:09–6:22	6:21–5:47	5:27	5:15	5:00	4:50 (1:55)	4:41 (1:52)	4:25 (1:46)
39	7:02–6:15	6:14–5:35	5:20	5:09	4:54	4:43 (1:53)	4:35 (1:50)	4:20 (1:44)
38	6:54–6:08	6:07–5:33	5:14	5:02	4:47	4:38 (1:51)	4:29 (1:47)	4:14 (1:42)
37	6:48–6:02	6:02–5:27	5:08	4:56	4:42	4:32 (1:48)	4:23 (1:45)	4:09 (1:40)
36	6:41–5:54	5:54–5:21	5:02	4:51	4:36	4:21 (1:46)	4:18 (1:43)	4:03 (1:38)
35	6:36–5:49	5:48–5:15	4:56	4:45	4:32	4:21 (1:44)	4:12 (1:41)	3:59 (1:36)
34	6:29–5:43	5:42–5:09	4:51	4:39	4:21	4:17 (1:42)	4:08 (1:39)	3:54 (1:34)
33	6:23–5:36	5:36–5:04	4:45	4:35	4:21	4:12 (1:40)	4:03 (1:37)	3.50 (1:32)
32	6:12–5:31	5:30–4:59	4:41	4:29	4:17	4:07 (1:38)	3:59 (1:35)	3:45 (1:30)
31	6:12–5:26	5:27–4:54	4:36	4:24	4:12	4:03 (1:37)	3:54 (1:34)	3:41 (1:29)

CONTINUES

TABLE 2b Find Your Target Pace Zones (pace per kilometer) CONTINUED

TPL	Recovery	Base Pace	26.2-Mile Pace	13.1-Mile Pace	10K Pace	5K Pace	3K Pace	1500-Meter Pace
30	6:05–5:21	5:20–4:50	4:32	4:20	4:08	3:59 (1:35)	3:50 (1:32)	3:37 (1:27)
29	6:00–5:17	5:16–4:44	4:21	4:16	4:03	3:54 (1:33)	3:47 (1:30)	3:33 (1:26)
28	5:54–5:11	5:11–4:40	4:22	4:11	4:00	3:51 (1:32)	3:42 (1:29)	3:30 (1:24)
27	5:50–5:07	5:06–4:36	4:18	4:07	3:56	3:47 (1:31)	3:39 (1:27)	3:26 (1:23)
26	5:46–5:02	5:02–4:32	4:14	4:03	3:51	3:44 (1:30)	3:35 (1:26)	3:23 (1:21)
25	5:42–4:58	4:57–4:27	4:10	3:59	3:48	3:40 (1:28)	3:32 (1:24)	3:19 (1:20)
24	5:37–4:54	4:53–4:23	4:06	3:56	3:45	3:36 (1:26)	3:29 (1:23)	3:16 (1:19)
23	5.33–4:50	4:49–4:20	4:03	3:52	3:41	3:33 (1:25)	3:26 (1:22)	3:13 (1:17)
22	5:29–4:45	4:45–4:16	3:59	3:44	3:38	3:30 (1:24)	3:23 (1:21)	3:10 (1:16)
21	5:26–4:42	4:41–4:11	3:56	3:45	3:35	3:27 (1:22)	3:18 (1:19)	3:08 (1:15)
20	5:18–4:38	4:38–4:08	3:52	3:42	3:32	3:24 (1:21)	3:16 (1:18)	3:05 (1:14)
19	5:14–4:34	4:33–4:05	3:44	3:39	3:29	3:21 (1:20)	3:13 (1:17)	3:02 (1:13)
18	5:11–4:31	4:30–4:02	3:46	3:35	3:26	3:18 (1:19)	3:11 (1:16)	2:59 (1:12)
17	5:08–4:27	4:21–3:59	3:43	3:32	3:23	3:15 (1:18)	3:08 (1:15)	2:57 (1:11)
16	5:04–4:24	4:23–3:56	3:40	3:30	3:21	3:13 (1:17)	3:05 (1:14)	2:54 (1:10)
15	5:01–4:20	4:20–3:53	3:36	3:27	3:17	3:11 (1:16)	3:02 (1:13)	2:52 (1:09)
14	4:57–4:17	4:17–3:50	3:34	3:24	3:15	3:08 (1:15)	3:00 (1:12)	2:50 (1:08)
13	4:54–4:14	4:12–3:47	3:31	3:21	3:12	3:06 (1:14)	2:58 (1:11)	2:48 (1:07)
12	4:51–4:11	4:10–3:44	3:29	3:18	3:10	3:03 (1:13)	2:56 (1:10)	2:45 (1:06)
11	4:48–4:08	4:07–3:42	3:26	3:16	3:08	3:01 (1:12)	2:53 (1:09)	2:43 (1:05)

TABLE 2b Find Your Target Pace Zones (pace per kilometer)

TPL	Recovery	Base Pace	26.2-Mile Pace	13.1-Mile Pace	10K Pace	5K Pace	3K Pace	1500-Meter Pace
10	4:42–4:05	4:05–3:39	3:24	3:14	3:06	2:59 (1:12)	2:51 (1:08)	2:41 (1:04)
9	4:39–4:02	4:02–3:36	3:21	3:12	3:03	2:56 (1:10)	2:49 (1:07)	2:39 (1:04)
8	4:36–3:59	3:59–3:33	3:18	3:09	3:01	2:54 (1:09)	2:47 (1:06)	2:37 (1:03)
7	4:34–3:57	3:56–3:31	3:16	3:07	2:59	2:52 (1:09.0)	2:45 (1:06)	2:35 (1:02)
6	4:31–3:53	3:53–3:29	3:14	3:05	2:57	2:50 (1:08)	2:42 (1:05)	2:33 (1:01)
5	4:28–3:51	3:50–3:27	3:06	3:02	2:55	2:48 (1:07)	2:41 (1:04)	2:32 (1:01)
4	4:21–3:44	3:48–3:24	3:09	3:01	2:53	2:47 (1:06)	2:39 (1:03)	2:30 (1:00)
3	4:23–3:45	3:45–3:22	3:07	2:59	2:51	2:44 (1:05)	2:37 (1:03)	2:27 (0:59)
2	4:21–3:44	3:43–3:20	3:05	2:56	2:50	2:42 (1:05)	2:36 (1:02)	2:26 (0:59)
1	4:19–3:42	3:41–3:18	3:03	2:54	2:48	2:41 (1:04)	2:29 (1:01)	2:24 (0:58)

Note: Numbers in parentheses are pace per 400m. For ease of use, the 400m time is calculated for 5K, 3K, and 1500m paces because intervals run at these faster paces are typically shorter in length. For example, a TPL 35 runner doing six 800m intervals at his or her 5K pace would be attempting to run each 800 as close to 3:28 as possible.

About the Author

Matt Fitzgerald is the author of several published and forthcoming books on fitness, nutrition, and weight loss, including *Runner's World Guide to Cross-Training* (2004), *The Cutting-Edge Runner* (2005), *Performance Nutrition for Runners* (2006), and *Triathlete Magazine's Essential Week-by-Week Training Guide* (2006). His first published work, *Triathlete Magazine's Complete Triathlon Book* (2003), now has 53,000 copies in print.

A prolific health and fitness journalist, Matt currently serves as senior editor of *Triathlete* and contributing editor of *Inside Triathlon*. As a freelancer, he writes regularly for such national publications as *Bicycling*, *Experience Life*, *Her Sports*, *Maxim*, *Men's Fitness*, *Men's Health*, *Outside*, *Runner's World*, *Stuff*, and *Triathlete* and for websites such as Active.com and Runner's World Online.

In addition to his work as a writer, Matt is a featured coach with Training Peaks, the leader in online training services for endurance athletes and coaches. Matt trains 10 to 20 hours per week and lives in San Diego with his wife.